Talking God

Talking God

Preaching to Contemporary Congregations

Albert R. Cutié

Morehouse Publishing
NEW YORK

Unless otherwise noted, the Scripture quotations contained herein are from the New Revised Standard Version Bible, copyright © 1989 by the Division of Christian Education of the National Council of Churches of Christ in the U.S.A. Used by permission. All rights reserved.

Morehouse Publishing, 19 East 34th Street, New York, NY 10016

Morehouse Publishing is an imprint of Church Publishing Incorporated.
www.churchpublishing.org

Cover design by Jenn Kopec, 2Pug Design
Typeset by PerfecType, Nashville, Tennessee

Library of Congress Cataloging-in-Publication Data
Names: Cutié, Albert, author.
Title: Talking God : preaching to contemporary congregations / Albert R.
    Cutié.
Description: New York : Morehouse Publishing, 2016. | Includes
    bibliographical references. | Description based on print version record
    and CIP data provided by publisher; resource not viewed.
Identifiers: LCCN 2016002187 (print) | LCCN 2015044771 (ebook) |
ISBN
    9780819232700 (ebook) | ISBN 9780819232694 (pbk.)
Subjects: LCSH: Preaching. | Communication—Religious aspects
—Christianity.
    | Christianity and culture.
Classification: LCC BV4211.3 (print) | LCC BV4211.3 .C88 2016
(ebook) | DDC
    251—dc23
LC record available at http://lccn.loc.gov/2016002187

Contents

Acknowledgments

Like good stewards of the manifold grace of God,
serve one another with whatever gift each of you has received
—1 PETER 4:10

My love and utmost gratitude goes to my wonderful wife, Ruhama. Through this long journey that included two pregnancies, two births, long nights in the library, travel to and from Sewanee, she has been my greatest supporter, along with our three precious children: Christian, Camila, and Albert. I love you.

To my mom and dad, thank you for raising me knowing the love of God, offering me a true example of Christian living, and always encouraging me in my education.

To the people of Church of the Resurrection in Biscayne Park and St. Benedict's in Plantation, Florida, your prayers and support throughout this process will always be treasured.

To our beloved Bishop Leo Frade, the third bishop of Southeast Florida, my unwavering gratefulness for your courageous leadership, for receiving me as a member of The Episcopal Church, and later, for welcoming me as a member of the clergy in your diocese. Ruhama and I will always be grateful to you and Diana for your incredible support. Likewise, to our beloved and newly instituted Bishop Peter Eaton, the fourth bishop of Southeast Florida, and his wife Kate. We are blessed to have you as part of our diocesan family and to share the gifts of life and ministry.

To the staff at the Duncan Conference Center (Diocese of Southeast Florida), where I am privileged to serve on the board of directors, I thank you for always providing me the quietest, absolutely peaceful, and most perfect setting for prayer, research, and writing. Your ministry of hospitality is a blessing to all!

A version of this book served as the thesis for my doctor of ministry degree from the School of Theology at Sewanee: The University of the South. A special word of thanks goes to those who provided me with significant wisdom, guidance, and much needed direction in the preparation and completion of that project: my thesis director, The Reverend Dr. William Brosend (Professor of Homiletics at the University of the South and Executive Director of the Episcopal Preaching Foundation); my second reader, The Reverend Peter Wallace (President and Executive Producer, Alliance for Christian Media, and host of "Day1"); Mr. James W. Dunkly (Librarian of the School of Theology, Associate

University Librarian, and Lecturer in New Testament at the University of the South); and my very dedicated copy editor, Dr. Cheryl J. Hill (Nova Southeastern University), a faithful member of St. Benedict's parish, where I am privileged to serve and attempt to preach the Gospel, applying just a few of the principles presented in this work. Special thanks to Nancy Bryan, Ryan Masteller, and the team at Church Publishing for helping this book come together. It is through your work and dedication that such a diversity of voices are heard—and read.

The Ongoing Impact of the Evolution of Our Media Culture

The single biggest problem in communication is the illusion that it has taken place.

—GEORGE BERNARD SHAW

For two millennia, Christians have gone to great lengths to fulfill what is commonly known as "The Great Commission," found in Mark 16:15, to "go preach the gospel to every creature." Countless men and women of every generation have made great sacrifices and often extraordinary efforts to announce the unique message of the Gospel—the saving message of our Lord Jesus Christ—throughout the world. Yet, while that message has not changed and its meaning remains timeless, the ways in which the Gospel is communicated and received are rapidly changing and evolving. This poses new challenges and new opportunities for all who are interested in the craft of preaching and communicating.

Given the explosion of new forms of media in the twentieth and early twenty-first centuries, the fundamental questions in our present context have increasingly become communication related. How is the church fulfilling its role as the most prominent "communicator" of the gospel and how effectively are we using the constantly evolving methods of communication? In a globalized world with immediate communication readily available almost universally, how is the church responding to the Lord's Great Commission to preach the gospel to "all creatures?" Are we really communicating with contemporary society and within its listening contexts, which are becoming increasingly more mobile (i.e. smart phones, tablets, watch phones, etc.) and accessible in all times and places? These questions can be overwhelming and even fear-provoking at times, yet these are the questions we must ask ourselves and the challenges we must embrace if we are to continue to aspire to be effective communicators of the Gospel.

Without seeking to be the bearer of *bad news*, all of the latest research regarding "Millennials" (also referred to as Generation Y) and others who comprise today's up-and-coming generations indicates that our varied religious traditions in the United States and other developed countries are not appealing to younger audiences or effectively communicating the message that we claim as sacred and essential to us.

However, we must go beyond evaluating new media developments and changes in the listening context in order to understand what changes in approach and methods may be necessary to connect with today's complex audiences. While much of the research one finds in this work is necessarily sociological in nature, our focus here is on the craft of preaching and the challenges at hand for those who seek to spread the Gospel in a sermon. We cannot deny that the craft of preaching—a message transmitted mostly by the spoken word and in the traditional context of the liturgy—remains at the very heart of the church's activity. Yet, while much has been written about the theology of communication and communications theory, the impact of new forms of media on the mission of Christ's church to preach the Gospel effectively has yet to be thoroughly measured and/or evaluated. As a matter of fact, it appears as though the more both church and communication experts write and speak about it, the more we realize that we are facing a David and Goliath phenomenon: this is a huge challenge for the church in our times. It is a reality we are only beginning to comprehend and whose evolution may very well be faster and greater than we can follow. Thus, the question becomes, "Will the church ever be able to address this immense task of effective contemporary communication?"

Perhaps one very real source of consolation for those who are intimidated by the immensity of constantly evolving and new technologies is that the preaching of the Gospel has always involved a very simple communications strategy:

a preacher and a congregation sitting before him or her waiting to hear a message. It is a method that seems standard and intransient. Regardless of whether that audience is a small group of people at a service in a nursing home, a massive congregation of thousands in a mega-church, or millions watching or listening through some form of media, preaching is still preaching. That is true. Yet, it is equally true that while each unique context for preaching influences the method and style used to deliver the message, the core experience of preaching seems to stay the same. Perhaps the one thing that is ultimately new or innovative in the craft of preaching is that we can no longer ignore the fact that developments in digital communications pose a series of new challenges to preachers and listeners alike, and that in the midst of those very real challenges there may be fantastic opportunities to create a better mechanism for the transmission and reception of the message. While we cannot deny that the way in which congregations receive and perceive the message preached has changed in the past few centuries, some will continue to subscribe to the theory that "the more things change, the more they stay the same" when it comes to the preaching of the Word of God. This could prove a dangerous route to take in the long-term. It is the route of apathy and comfort, a perspective we hear in many of our communities which asserts, "but we have always done it that way."

The rapid evolution of new forms of media in the context of the church and its mission remind me of the old hardware stores I often visited with my father and grandfathers as a little boy. In a matter of decades, even after years and years providing personal care and attention to their customers, the big department and new mega-stores came in and wiped them out. It was devastating to those dedicated local business owners and obviously devastating to their most loyal clients, but they closed because the world around them changed. Their new customer base did not respond to their approach; as good and as dedicated as it was, it did not keep up with the change that surrounded them. This is perhaps where the "buy local" movement is beginning to fill a void left by those smaller, more personal buying experiences of the past. This trend could be good news for churches that feel they are too small to compete with mega-churches and their seemingly endless resources.

The challenge for the church today is not dissimilar to the challenge faced by those hardware stores. We too must be ready to ask if the twenty-first-century church is responding to this on-going media revolution by seeking to understand the present day "listening context" and the often overwhelming media culture in which it is called to preach. Must preachers and teachers of the Word of God evolve in style and practice in order to continue being effective communicators of the Gospel message? Has the world changing around us changed our methodology or our message?

My hope is that this book will help us begin to understand how preaching can more effectively meet the needs of our changing world, proclaiming the Gospel to present-day circumstances. Every area of communication is evolving, affecting the way we transmit and receive information. We will compare changes in preaching styles within our contemporary context. Exploring this may allow us to learn from preachers in the Christian tradition who have captivated thousands successfully, largely as a result of their unique communicative styles. Effective speaking styles and how they continue to evolve will also be reviewed.

Finally, we will consider my own simple and nonscientific survey of preachers and congregants (listeners of sermons) who responded to questions regarding contemporary preaching, with the hope that this will help us to pause and think as a rapidly changing media culture affects our desire to carry out God's work in today's world.

While many today use the terms "sermon" and "homily" interchangeably, they are not always understood as being the same. Traditionally, sermons were considered speeches on some particular Christian doctrine or a discourse on morality, while homilies have historically been associated with the preaching event within the liturgy, inviting believers to apply the biblical message to their daily living. Most Anglicans/ Episcopalians and Roman Catholics are accustomed to hearing the term "homily," while other Christian denominations use the term "sermon" almost exclusively. In this book, I have used the term "sermon" in a very broad way, seeking to embrace both tendencies within the Body of Christ.

CHAPTER 1

The Historical Evolution of the Sermon

For just as you are hungry to listen to me,
so too I am hungry to preach to you.
—St. John Chrysostom

Not unlike any other method or system of communication, the sermon has changed and evolved throughout the centuries. In the early church, many sermons were "apologias" (a Greek term referring to the defense of a particular Christian teaching or doctrine), usually intense theological explanations of a topic being debated or defined by the early Christians. The witness of Justin Martyr (c. 150 AD) in his famous letter to the Roman Emperor, Antoninus Pius, describes those early Christian sermons by saying that the "presider of the assembly speaks to us; he urges everyone to imitate the examples of virtue we have heard in the readings."[1] This is an early and rare description of a sermon in the second century of Christianity within the context of Sunday worship. Yet, we get a lot from that brief statement. We are told that there was a preacher who spoke to the assembly, and that there was an exhortation inviting specific changes to be made in the lives of those gathered as a result of the proclamation. It is fair to say that the craft of preaching has always involved a preacher and an assembly trying to comprehend how best to understand and apply the meaning of the Word of God for the living out of our Christian lives. The fact that there is a preacher and there are listeners is perhaps one of the only aspects of preaching and proclamation that will not be radically subjected to the communications revolution taking place around us.

However, when we take a look back in time we discover that the most renowned testimonies of the first centuries of Christianity were primarily focused on the martyrdoms of significant figures who had a great impact on the life of that primitive church. Certainly the stories of Perpetua, Felicity, and other martyrs were considered a powerful witness that led those around them in the Christian community to embrace the Gospel and live the message of the Word of God.[2] The witness of these stories was a powerful tool

---

1. Justin Martyr, 150 AD.
2. Paul Scott Wilson, *A Concise History of Preaching* (Nashville, TN: Abingdon Press, 1992), 30–34.

within the early Christian church, which found itself at odds with a hostile cultural milieu.

In this sense, one could say that the Christian sermon has gone full-circle, with popular preachers of the twentieth and twenty-first centuries focusing a great deal of attention (in their sermons) on their own personal stories of pain, abuse, addiction, and other human dramas, which may make their message more appealing—or even more credible—to contemporary listeners. In the early church, for some it was the witness of martyrdom that made the Gospel attractive. While it is certainly a stretch (i.e. martyrdom vs. stories of personal strife) one cannot ignore the strong connection between personal testimony, witness, and experience in both the primitive church and in some contemporary Christian traditions. One could say that many pastors today are actually recognized for those personal journeys and often use those narratives in their preaching much more so than their level of education or knowledge of theology.

In order to go deeper into our understanding of the changes within the craft of preaching as a result of our media culture, this chapter will focus on the evolution of sermons in the post-Reformation era (after 1685). We'll do that by looking briefly at a theologically and denominationally diverse group of preachers who can be categorized as "iconic" figures in the most recent centuries of Christian history. The first two lived in a time when, apart from print media, technology did not provide for much more than the traditional pulpit and the spoken word. Yet, with the dawn of radio and television in the twentieth century, others became among the most influential people of our time. By looking at these sermons and the well-known and transformational individuals who preached them, I believe we will be able to discern the evolution that has already occurred and the developments that will continue to take place in preaching. Rather than pretending to use these six preachers as some sort of case study, we will look directly at each specific style used to preach the Christian Gospel and the effect their surroundings and particular cultural milieu had on the message they proclaimed and continue to share today.

John Wesley (1703–1791)

John Wesley understood the apostolic mission of the church in the most radical way and put it into practice in the most literal way. The very origin of the word "apostle" (in Greek *apostollein*) refers to one who is "sent" or to actually "send away." Wesley, his brother Charles (the renowned author of over five thousand hymns), and the great Anglican preacher and mentor to Wesley, George Whitefield, took the Gospel to the streets. As some of the first in England to promote preaching outdoors in the eighteenth century, they were harshly criticized and persecuted for initiating this unpopular practice.

Wesley and his colleagues had begun the practice of public preaching and what would evolve to become what we now call "revivals" as a result of their association with the Holy Club in Oxford.[3] The Holy Club was dedicated to the pursuit of holiness, originating what would become known as the "Holiness Movement" with their specific mix of religious study, piety, and service that would eventually lead to the establishment of Methodist societies (although Wesley would declare himself an Anglican until his death).[4] There is little doubt that in Wesley's unique style and in the movement he helped to lead, something new was taking place. Wesley and those who became adherents of his method were taking Christianity back out into the streets, beyond the walls of the church. The step of taking the sermon from the context of the traditional indoor pulpit and making it accessible to any who might want to listen on the street was not a new method, but an application of an old, forgotten method—the one used by prophets and apostles of biblical times, who spent their time beyond the confines of physical structures and/or religious buildings. One could say that those outdoor revivals of the eighteenth century were the "mass media" of their times. It was certainly the only way to reach thousands of people, gathered in a single space to hear God's message.

I believe this open air or "field preaching," as it was called, led Wesley to become a truly effective communicator among the people of his time. He possessed a simplicity and directness not common among his colleagues who

---

3. Wilson, *A Concise History of Preaching*, 131.
4. Ibid., 133.

preached in more formal indoor settings. This is evident
from the preface of Wesley's first publication of sermons in
1746 in which he states:

> I design plain truth for plain people; therefore, to
> set purpose, I abstain from all nice and philosophi-
> cal speculations; from all perplexed and intricate rea-
> sonings; and, as far as possible, from even the show
> of learning, unless in sometimes citing the original
> Scripture. I labour to avoid all words which are not
> easy to be understood, all which are not used in com-
> mon life; and, in particular, those kinds of technical
> terms that so frequently occur in Bodies of Divinity;
> those modes of speaking which men of reading are
> intimately acquainted with, but to common people are
> an unknown tongue.[5]

Here, Wesley the street preacher is articulating his case for
what guides his preaching style: a desire to communicate
the Gospel effectively to all people, both those familiar
with theological concepts and (mostly) those who were
not. In the eyes of too many of the churchmen of his day,
this enthusiastic and popular approach posed a real threat,
a danger to the dignified style of preaching most ascribed to.
In spite of the opposition he faced from colleagues in the

---

5. Edward H. Sugden, ed., *Wesley's Standard Sermons Consisting of 44
Discourses Published in Four Volumes*, vol. 1 (London: Epworth Press,
1956), preface.

church, Wesley continued to motivate the listeners of his outdoor sermons to be faithful in their attendance at worship and to the reception of the sacraments. While he was indeed an innovative preacher, he by no means discouraged the traditional practices of Christianity and regular church attendance.[6] However, as several critics have noted, none of his published sermons put much emphasis on church attendance.

What we do find explicitly present in almost all of Wesley's sermons is his passion, personal style, and approach. Obviously, they do not contain the language, speech patterns, or approach we are accustomed to hearing, but they very much represent his eighteenth-century context and the use of the sermon to express doctrinal and theological perspectives. At the same time, one can see that there is a very personal and direct message being transmitted. This typical Wesleyan approach is evident in his 1746 sermon on "Justification by Faith":

> Thou ungodly one, who hearest or readest these words! Thou vile, helpless, miserable sinner! I charge thee before God, the Judge of all, go straight unto him, with all thy ungodliness. Take heed thou destroy not thy own soul by pleading thy righteousness, more or less. Go as altogether ungodly, guilty, lost, destroyed, deserving and dropping into hell; and thou shalt then

6. Wilson, *A Concise History of Preaching*, 133.

find favour in his sight, and know that he justifieth the ungodly. As such thou shalt be brought unto the "blood of sprinkling," as an undone, helpless, damned sinner. Thus "look unto Jesus!" There is "the Lamb of God," who "taketh away thy sins!" Plead thou no works, no righteousness of thine own! No humility, contrition, sincerity! In nowise. That were, in very deed, to deny the Lord that bought thee. No: Plead thou, singly, the blood of the covenant, the ransom paid for thy proud, stubborn, sinful soul. Who art thou, that now seest and feelest both thine inward and outward ungodliness? Thou art the man! I want thee for my Lord! I challenge "thee" for a child of God by faith! The Lord hath need of thee. Thou who feelest thou art just fit for hell, art just fit to advance his glory; the glory of his free grace, justifying the ungodly and him that worketh not. O come quickly! Believe in the Lord Jesus; and thou, even thou, art reconciled to God.[7]

The passion and style in Wesley's "Justification" sermon is evident. While some of the language seems rather harsh to contemporary ears, a zealous and energetic preaching style is clear even in the written text. Yet, as we read these sermons, one wonders how it was possible for thousands of

---

7. "Sermons of John Wesley" (Sermon #5) "Justification by Faith" accessed October 15, 2014, http://wesley.nnu.edu/john-wesley/ the-sermons-of-john-wesley-1872-edition/sermon-5-justification -by-faith.

people to have heard and understood these outdoor preachers and their elaborate phrases without benefit of microphones or public address systems. The answer provided by several scholars is that preaching was carefully delivered with a kind of voice that was "close to singing,"[8] allowing their voices to carry and be heard at much greater distances. This style should not be compared to the almost gimmicky shouting we hear from so many of today's television preachers, but a true instrument which captivated large audiences and allowed the message to be heard and understood. The projection and clarity of Wesley's voice accompanied the passion with which the message was proclaimed. To illustrate this point, we look to Wesley's mentor and another great outdoor preacher, George Whitefield, who was once asked for permission to publish his sermons. Whitefield responded, "Well, I have no inherent objection, if you like, but you will never be able to put on the printed page the lightning and the thunder."[9]

To Wesley's contemporaries, the content, power, and delivery of the spoken word had great value and were integral to the craft of preaching. Once those sermons were written, which unfortunately is the only way we can experience them today, they lose a great deal of their personality. Perhaps today, as the traditional context of worship

8. Wilson, *A Concise History of Preaching*, 137.
9. D. Martyn Lloyd-Jones, *Preaching and Preachers* (London, Hodder & Stoughton, 1971), 58.

through the emerging church and other movements, we can look to Wesley, Whitefield, and others who brought crowds together in outdoor settings and brought the Gospel to the people.

Contemporary preachers can surely benefit from Wesley's perseverance in listening to the voice of God within, seeking new ways to proclaim the message of the kingdom. Although it was not considered decent for a man of the cloth to go out and do "street preaching," that is precisely what Wesley did. He did all this without microphones, video cameras, or any type of equipment. His only instruments were the Gospel, his voice, and his God-given courage to break the mold and take the saving message of God beyond buildings and the pulpits found within them. John Wesley's ministry as preacher and pastor offers us examples of innovation and courage—and the results that can come from using those gifts.

Charles H. Spurgeon (1834–1892)

Charles Spurgeon was known as the "Prince of Preachers." A Baptist preacher who served as the pastor of London's largest congregation, he never attended a Bible College or any kind of seminary. He received harsh criticism for this throughout his life, but especially at the beginning of his ministry when, at the age of nineteen, he took over the renowned New Park Street Baptist Church where he was often referred to as the "boy preacher."[10] Regardless, Spurgeon was privileged to preach at some of the largest venues in London and was known to have preached to over ten million people in his lifetime. Furthermore, it is important to note that there is no other Christian author—living or dead—who has more material in print, even more than a century after his death.[11] His impact was, and continues to be, enormous in many Christian circles.

Spurgeon considered himself a hard-core Calvinist, yet his theology never seemed to get in the way of his popular appeal. His emphasis was connecting with people, and his powerful voice, theatrical style, and humor helped him to accomplish that. On the occasion of Spurgeon's first Sunday at New Park Street Church, he had eighty persons in his congregation. On his last Sunday there, after thirty-seven years, he had the largest evangelical congregation in the world: at that time over 5,300 members.[12] What was evident from his preaching and life was that he possessed a contagious spirituality, and his ability to preach in a way that was accessible to all made him a very powerful communicator, always in command of his message. He did not write out his sermons,

---

10. "The Secrets of Spurgeon's Preaching," *Christianity Today* (2005), accessed November 1, 2014, http://www.christianitytoday.com/ct/2005/juneweb-only/52.0.html.
11. Ibid.
12. Ibid.

and those who observed him claim that most often he took to the pulpit with him only a very brief outline written on the back of an envelope or piece of paper.

In one of his sermons, expressing his personal style and approach, he spoke of how humbled he was by the incredible sacredness of the task he considered preaching to be:

Often, when I come in at the door and my eyes fall on this vast congregation, I feel a tremor go through me to think that I should have to speak to you all and be, in some measure, accountable for your future state. Unless I preach the Gospel faithfully and with all my heart, your blood will be required at my hands. Do not wonder, therefore, that when I am weak and sick, I feel my head swim when I stand up to speak to you, and my heart is often faint within me. But I do have this joy at the back of it all—God does set many sinners free in this place! Some people reported that I was mourning that there were no conversions. Brothers and Sisters, if you were all to be converted tonight, I should mourn for the myriads outside! That is true, but I praise the Lord for the many who are converted here. When I came last Tuesday to see converts, I had 21 whom I was able to propose to the Church—and it will be the same next Tuesday, I do not doubt. God is saving souls! I am not preaching in vain. I am not despondent about that matter—liberty is given to the captives and there will be liberty for some of them, tonight! I wonder who it will be? Some of you

young women over yonder, I trust. Some who have
dropped in here, tonight, for the first time. Oh, may this
first opportunity of your hearing the Word in this place
be the time of beginning a new life which shall never
end—a life of holiness, a life of peace with God![13]

In spite of the fact that Spurgeon spoke before multitudes,
he never lost a sense of the personal pastoral connection
with his flock. There is a powerfully evident humility in this
preacher, his great preaching ability accompanied by strong
pastoral care, something often missing in contemporary
popular preachers who often make themselves inaccessible.
Living a century later than John Wesley, it is apparent that
Spurgeon's sermons are much less formal in their tone and
language than Wesley's. Spurgeon was certainly among the
first media preachers, even before the existence of television and radio, because of his effective and considerable use
of print media. Spurgeon sold twenty thousand copies of
his sermons each week. They were translated into twenty
languages, and he collected his sermons into sixty-three volumes. Today, Spurgeon's sermons are considered the largest collection of books by any Christian author in history.
His impact in the nineteenth century was truly remarkable.
One lesson Spurgeon offers to today's preachers is that sermons may have a life of their own, and if we value what

---

13. "Notable Quotes of Charles Spurgeon," Sermon #2371 (1894),
accessed October 25, 2014, http://www.spurgeongems.org.

we preach, we may wish to make it available beyond the preaching moment through some form of media. How many times have you heard, "That was a great sermon"? Yet, often after we have been inspired and touched by such a message, the mind moves on to other things and the content of the sermon may not stay with us as we would wish it to. Spurgeon understood this and, thanks to the availability of his sermons, we are still talking about them today. Important messages should not be easily forgotten.

Fulton J. Sheen (1895–1979)

When we hear the term "televangelists" we may think first of some of the horror stories surrounding famous preachers with extravagant lifestyles who were not always models of Christian living. Yet, the person often referred to as "the first televangelist" was a deeply spiritual and brilliant Roman Catholic bishop whose presence coincided with the dawn of television and whose impact on American society went well beyond his own religious tradition. Billy Graham often referred to Bishop Fulton J. Sheen as "the greatest communicator of the twentieth century," and *TIME Magazine* called him "the microphone of God."[14] For those of us familiar with his work, it is truly difficult to find anyone with whom

---

14. "Religion: The Microphone of God," obituary of Fulton J. Sheen, *Time*, December 24, 1979, accessed December 10, 2014, http://content.time.com/time/magazine/article/0,9171,947144,00.html.

to compare him. The uniqueness of his style and magnitude of his eloquence is truly unparalleled.

Fulton J. Sheen started as an extremely popular host on radio in 1930, where he had millions of listeners. For a period of time, he received thousands of daily letters from his faithful audience. Shortly after the dawn of television in 1951, he had a show on prime-time national television, coincided in the same time slot with the great Milton Berle on another network. As a competitor to "Uncle Miltie," Sheen soon earned the nickname of "Uncle Fultie" from his legions of viewers. He realized his audience was diverse, and unlike many other television and radio preachers, he understood he was reaching people with a universal message that applied to people of all faith traditions. In his autobiography, Sheen states,

> When I began television nationally and on a commercial basis, I was no longer talking in the name of the church and under the sponsorship of bishops. The new method had to be more ecumenical and directed to Catholics, Protestant, Jews, and all men of good will. It was no longer a presentation of Christian doctrine but rather a reasoned approach to it beginning with something that was common to the audience. Hence, during those television years, the subjects ranged from communism, to art, to science, to humor, aviation, war, etc.[15]

---

15. Fulton J. Sheen, *Treasure in Clay: The Autobiography of Archbishop Fulton J. Sheen* (New York: Image, 1982).

Sheen's particular charisma allowed him to reach millions on non-religious media with a message that never came across as "churchy," while still communicating the Gospel effectively. He was responsible, as God's accessible and gifted instrument, for the conversions of several prominent public figures to Christianity, baptizing them into the church. Bishop Sheen had the gift of making Christianity appealing; he was a true master at using the immense power of the media for this kind of "indirect evangelism" (as I like to call it). He understood that the very presence of a priest on secular/commercial television and radio was enough to make the people wonder about spiritual and religious matters, without a sermon always being preached.

Sheen had a classical education and was well versed in several biblical and modern languages. He earned two doctorates: one in philosophy and another in theology. This master communicator was the author of seventy-three books, many of which became classics. He was ecumenical and developed ties with the likes of Billy Graham, several popular rabbis, and a host of other religious leaders even before the Second Vatican Council's Decree on Ecumenism. While Sheen was an academic, his education and theoretical thoroughness never distanced him from the importance of effectively reaching his audience. On the contrary, he was able to speak in a way that easily connected with all. His programs were not a pulpit in front of a congregation, but a conversational style lecture, where the dynamic bishop caught everyone's attention as he spoke on issues of the day and topics of human interest. The very title of his program said it all: "Life is Worth Living." His programs were all about life, decades before "self-help" would even become a recognizable genre.

When it came to preaching in the context of the liturgy, he was equally engaging. Here, there was no camera to look into with his piercing eyes, but he looked into the assembly in a way that each person felt he was speaking to them. His preaching style was more formal than what is customary today, but his personal style kept his formality accessible as he connected the message to his listeners. Bishop Sheen had a way of combining anecdotes, humor, and constant biblical references seamlessly. He was a Christ-centered preacher and spoke of the Lord in a way that made the Gospel come alive; he mesmerized audiences and congregations while challenging them never to be afraid of responding to their Christian calling. The cross of Christ was one of his constant references, but it was always in the framework and at the service of hope. Unlike some Christian preachers, Sheen did not focus on the cross in order to emphasize the pain but to emphasize the hope of resurrection. In one of his popular Lenten missions he said,

Love does not kill pain, but it diminishes it . . . . As Christians we have one law: Good Friday and Easter.

Nothing is ever accomplished that is worthwhile without some self-denial and mortification. If you have a cross, bear it. It is his! And you'll be glad of it and for it someday. Your salvation is assured.[16]

Like so many of the preachers in this chapter, Bishop Sheen was criticized and treated harshly by some within the church. His own archbishop in New York, Cardinal Spellman, did everything possible to get him out of the diocese after they had a disagreement about the proper use of mission funds. When the Pope sided with Sheen, the Cardinal seemed to use his power to maneuver for Sheen to be appointed Bishop of Rochester, placing him as far away from Manhattan as possible. Sheen was never invited to preach at St. Patrick's Cathedral again during Spellman's lifetime. He had to settle for the tiny St. Agnes Church a few blocks away, where the street (East 43rd Street) is now named after him.[17] Two months prior to his death and with Spellman now long gone, Sheen was present at St. Patrick's when he was embraced by Pope John Paul II during his first pastoral visit to the United States.

16. Bishop Fulton J. Sheen "Our Cross," sermon preached at a Lenten Mission, accessed November 1, 2014, https://www.youtube.com/watch?v=vkEBsVZBijg.

17. Patricia Kossman "Remembering Fulton Sheen," *America*, December 6, 2004, accessed November 15, 2014, http://americamagazine.org/issue/511/article/remembering-fulton-sheen.

The Pope said to Sheen, "You have written and spoken well of the Lord Jesus Christ. You are a loyal son of the Church . . . ."[18]

Contemporary preachers in a pluralistic society must be more and more willing to communicate in ways that reach beyond their own faith tradition. This in no way means that we disregard the gospel or down-play our fidelity to Christian doctrine Yet, what we can all learn from Sheen was his great ability to preach and teach audiences beyond his own tradition, motivated by the conviction of the universality of God's love—a message that goes beyond every human boundary. One of the characteristics we see in Fulton J. Sheen that calls for our reflection as preachers is the authenticity of our interest in communicating to the larger world, without compromising our faith. Sheen enthralled his listeners because he offered significant content, masterful delivery, and his unique personal style. Above all, he was an effective communicator, and indeed, for millions, he became "the microphone of God." Perhaps his greatest challenge for preachers is his innate understanding that weak communications skills can compromise the presentation of the strongest theology.

18. "Biography of Venerable Fulton Sheen," accessed November 15, 2014, http://www.actorschapel.org/Biography-Venerable-Fulton-Sheen.

Billy Graham (1918–)

For decades, when people in the United States thought of
a "national preacher," they thought of Billy Graham. Since
the late 1940s, Graham and the evangelistic organization
he founded created large gatherings of people under tents
and in stadiums as Graham preached the Gospel and issued
altar calls to invite those present to accept Christ in their
lives. Regardless of his critics and those who try to down-
play his legacy, there is little doubt that Rev. Graham is still
considered to be one of world's greatest representatives of
Christianity and a powerful voice. He has preached to more
than 215 million persons through faith rallies and revivals in
185 countries worldwide.[19]

Like Sheen, Graham spent much of his preaching time
making references to the problems and issues that were
considered pressing to believers and non-believers alike in
the twentieth century including the Cold War, communism,
and the moral decline in society since the 1960s. These
issues and his biblical perspective on them made Graham's
preaching particularly effective in a country often hungry
for a kind of moral compass and spiritual leadership perceived as absent from public life. Graham's friendship with
presidents and other public figures over the years has also
significantly affected his credibility and prominence in

---

19. Billy Graham Evangelistic Association Figures, accessed October
10, 2014, http://billygraham.org/about/biographies/billy-graham/.

American society. He has appeared in Gallup's list of "Most Admired Men" fifty-eight times, more than any other person on the planet.[20]

Graham's preaching style is not particularly creative or dynamic compared to many contemporary preachers, but he does come across as strongly authoritative while truly authentic, often repeating the phrase "the Bible says" and quoting Scripture passages to support his points during his preaching. His style is reminiscent of the sermons often associated with American mainstream denominations in the middle years of the previous century.

Very few religious leaders have had the spiritual and moral impact on the United States which can be attributed to the Reverend Graham. This has been apparent on numerous occasions, but perhaps never as obvious as it was during his moving sermon at the Cathedral Church of Saint Peter and Paul—popularly known as the National Cathedral—in Washington, D.C., where he addressed the nation shortly after the devastating attacks of September 11, 2001. On that special day of Prayer and Remembrance, in his sermon before the nation's leaders, Graham said:

> The Bible says that He is "the God of all comfort, who comforts us in all our troubles." No matter how hard

20. Gallup Poll results published in December 2014, accessed January 3, 2015, http://www.gallup.com/poll/180365/barack-obama-hillary -clinton-extend-run-admired.aspx?version=print.

we try words simply cannot express the horror, the shock, and the revulsion we all feel over what took place in this nation on Tuesday morning. September 11 will go down in our history as a day to remember. Today we say to those who masterminded this cruel plot, and to those who carried it out, that the spirit of this nation will not be defeated by their twisted and diabolical schemes. Someday those responsible will be brought to justice, as President Bush and our Congress have so forcefully stated. But today we especially come together in this service to confess our need of God. We've always needed God from the very beginning of this nation but today we need Him especially. We're facing a new kind of enemy. We're involved in a new kind of warfare and we need the help of the Spirit of God. The Bible's words are our hope: "God is our refuge and strength, an ever present help in trouble. Therefore we will not fear, though the earth give way and the mountains fall into the heart of the sea" (Psalm 46:1, 2, NIV). But how do we understand something like this? Why does God allow evil like this to take place? Perhaps that is what you are asking now. You may even be angry at God. I want to assure you that God understands those feelings that you may have. We've seen so much on our television, and hear on our radio, stories that bring tears to our eyes and make us all feel a sense of anger. But God can be trusted, even when life seems at its darkest. But what are some of the lessons we can learn? First, we are reminded of the mystery and reality of evil. I have been asked on hundreds of times in my life why God allows tragedy and suffering. I have to confess that I really do not know the answer totally, even to my own satisfaction. I have to accept, by faith, that God is sovereign, and He is a God of love and mercy and compassion in the midst of suffering. The Bible says God is not the author of evil. It speaks of evil as a "mystery." In 2 Thessalonians 2:7 it talks about the mystery of iniquity. The Old Testament prophet Jeremiah said, "The heart is deceitful above all things and beyond cure. Who can understand it?" He asked that question, "Who can understand it?" And that is one reason we each need God in our lives. The lesson of this event is not only about the mystery of iniquity and evil, but secondly, it is a lesson about our need for each other.[21]

In spite of the countless tent and stadium rallies since 1949 and the days of ongoing national and international crusades, I believe moments like this will be Graham's most lasting legacy: those moments when he preached the Gospel and comforted an entire nation and its leaders. Graham offered a spiritual sense of security when it was

---

21. The Rev. Billy Graham, sermon at the National Cathedral in Washington, D.C., on the Day of Remembrance for 9/11, September 14, 2001.

most difficult to have hope or faith or to think about God. His preaching will be a memorable part of American history.

Perhaps the most important thing contemporary preachers and leaders can learn from Graham is the importance of incarnational preaching—the ability to speak to the reality that is before us in a way that brings biblical images, examples, and truths to the forefront of the particular dilemma or tragedy most present in people's minds. We do preaching a great disservice when it is not incarnational and connected to the needs and interests of the listeners. Just as Jesus became flesh, the incarnational centrality of our lives as Christians, so must the message preached become flesh in the midst of today's human realities if the Gospel is to be understood as relevant.

Joyce Meyer (1943–)

I chose Joyce Meyer as one of our iconic preachers, not because of any affinity to her brand of theology or her interpretation of Scripture, but because she embodies so much of what the craft of preaching in the twenty-first century has become for a growing number of Christian clergy. Meyer is a combination of spiritual guru, preacher, counselor, self-help life coach, and powerfully effective communicator, all in one. She goes beyond the traditional televangelist persona and engages her audiences with her particular charisma and style. While many of Meyer's preaching, teaching, and public speaking events are marketed to women, she is equally effective with male audiences.

Joyce Meyer has mastered the art of preaching far beyond the religious or denominational affiliations of her listeners, and her messages are filled with biblical references while never seeming religious or "churchy" in tone. Though she was once a Lutheran, she became the associate pastor at a non-denominational church for several years before resigning to start her own ministry. Meyer often refers to "church folks," the rigidity of religious institutions, and the people by whom she felt mistreated when she worked for a particular church. Even this message resonates with many of her listeners, as so many individuals feel alienated and disenfranchised from the organized religious institutions of their upbringing. Meyer also often shares her experiences of sexual abuse by her father and other forms of abuse by her first husband, which permits her to have an almost immediate connection and credibility with those who have suffered emotional and physical abuse of various types. Not unlike her colleague in the media world, Oprah Winfrey (who early in her career shared painful details about her abusive past), Meyer has mastered the ability to use her experiences of adversity to help others who may have suffered similar experiences. This makes her more than a preacher of the Gospel to many women and men; she has become a kind of "spiritual hero" who, because of her ability to conquer the pain of her past, is now a living witness, worthy of imitation.

Meyer is an example of the ways in which sermons have evolved into a more personal and testimony-driven form of communication over the past decades. Like other contemporary preachers, Meyer offers a no-nonsense message of hope through her preaching, teaching, conferences, and books, resulting in a huge media-empire. This self-help/biblical style is quickly becoming what is being heard in many of the new "non-denominational" Christian churches in our times and from a number of prominent televangelists.

One of Meyer's recent sermons focused on a recurring theme of hers: how we deal with our feelings. She said,

> I certainly remember lots of times in my life when people asked me why I was being so harsh. I didn't realize that I was. I just had a lot going on and felt pressured, so the pressure came through in harsh voice tones. That didn't excuse my bad behavior, but it was the root of the problem. I am very thankful I know the Word of God and have Him in my life to help and comfort me. But a lot of difficult people don't have that. I have had to work very hard with the Holy Spirit for the ability to act on God's Word when people are rude . . . instead of merely reacting with a behavior that matches or tops theirs. Jesus teaches us how to respond to those who treat us well and those who do not *(see Luke 6:32–35)*. If you are in a situation that requires you to be with one of these hard-to-get-along-with people every day, I urge you to pray for them

instead of reacting emotionally to them. Our prayers open a door for God to work through.[22]

It is plain to see that this preacher's message is light on theology and heavy on practical advice for Christian living; perhaps this very accessibility makes her preaching appealing. Meyer has managed to bring together a personal approach to preaching and teaching with a sense of reverence for God's Word and its practical applications to daily living, which is explosively popular. She often is heard shying away from the title "televangelist" and prefers to be referred to as a "Practical Bible Teacher." However, her impact on the craft of preaching is immense. I am intrigued by her captivating style and authenticity as a communicator of the Gospel. In observing Meyer, I appreciate her consistency in delivery and persona, regardless of setting or format.

Contemporary preachers can learn from Meyer the need to bring more of our own humanity into our preaching: our personality, humor, creativity, personal experiences, and so forth. All of those aspects of who we are can be used by God in a way that will enhance our connection with those to whom we preach. From Meyer we learn that effectively connecting with your audience can be the difference in whether or not the message is heard. Meyer is, above all,

22. Joyce Meyer "God's Word vs. Your Feelings," accessed November 20, 2014, http://www.joycemeyer.org/articles/ea.aspx?article=gods_word _vs_your_feelings.

a wonderfully gifted story-teller and "connector" of God's message to the reality and problems of everyday living.

Michael Curry (1953–)

Michael Curry was elected the twenty-seventh Presiding Bishop of The Episcopal Church in July 2015; he is undoubtedly one of the most noted and recognized Anglican preachers and speakers today. With his charisma, energy, and style Curry could be a popular television preacher. He is a dedicated ecumenist, an active bishop, and above all, a feature of many lists of favorite preachers. Curry "has a national preaching and teaching ministry, having been featured on *Day 1* (formerly known as *The Protestant Hour*) and as a frequent speaker at conferences around the country. He has received honorary degrees from Sewanee and Yale."[23] As a result of his great ability as a preacher and communicator, Bishop Curry had become one of the most recognized spokespersons for The Episcopal Church long before his election to the role of Presiding Bishop.

Curry's personal dynamic style, straightforwardness, and his special gift with words and images are among the many qualities that contribute to his recognition as an outstanding preacher. Curry connects Scriptures with the most pressing contemporary issues. As William Brosend points out

23. Biographical page of The Rt. Rev. Michael Curry, accessed January 20, 2015, http://day1.org/280-the_rt_rev_michael_curry.

in *The Preaching of Jesus*, referring to the sermon delivered by Bishop Curry at the 2003 General Convention of The Episcopal Church (known as one of the most tumultuous gatherings in the denomination's history):

> Excellent sermons frequently share one thing in common: a transparent structure, whether the preacher planned it or not. The really good ones do not seem to need to plan it; they think that way. My later experience with sermons by Bishop Curry suggests that the clear structure of this sermon was no accident, or more precisely, it was the accident of design.[24]

Curry's preaching style is like listening to one's favorite jazz tune with series of improvisation riffs and tempos coming together in a coherent way. One cannot help but feel captivated by the energy in his voice and contagious enthusiasm for the biblical message. To highlight Brosend's point, what one experiences in Bishop Curry's sermons is indeed, "the accident of design." Perhaps this is why Curry's own understanding of sermon structure and preparation is so deeply incarnational: it is where structure, message, and reality come together. In his own words:

> The Word comes to life in the world. When preparing a sermon, the preacher needs to study the word and

---

24. William Brosend, *The Preaching of Jesus: Gospel Proclamation Then and Now* (Louisville: Westminster John Knox, 2010), 95.

hit the streets to see that Word lived out today . . . .
It's only out of the chemistry of bringing all that stuff
together that something worth saying, that actually has
the gravity of God's Word and that has the reality of
life as it gets lived somehow brought together—that's
incarnation. . . . That's where preaching happens.[25]

Contemporary preachers can learn from Curry's structure in preparing and thinking about the special impact
of the Word to be proclaimed. Those involved in the craft
of preaching can all learn from his "accident of design,"
never forgetting to "hit the streets" by connecting the biblical message with the realities on people's minds. Curry
reminds us that the one place Christianity may be losing
most of its relevance is precisely in the pulpit. To "hit the
streets" in sermon preparation is to move beyond the theological interpretation of scripture and offer the opportunity for transformation. Too often, preaching becomes an
eloquently presented set of ideas disconnected from each
other, and thus, disconnected from listeners and their daily
lives. Curry's style demonstrates that those in mainstream
denominations can indeed preach eloquently-organized sermons that bring together "all that stuff" (biblical exegesis,
sound structure, provocative and relevant content, effective

---

25. Michael Curry, "Preaching Moment 271: Michael Curry,"
accessed January 25, 2015, http://www.workingpreacher.org/craft
.aspx?post=2638.

delivery, and other things) to proclaim God's Word effectively and in a way that transforms people's lives.

Study Questions

1. As we look at historical sermons, what qualities seem to make a preacher unique and extraordinary? Is the biblical message enriched or diminished by a preacher's unique style?
2. What can today's preachers learn from the style and unique characteristics of outstanding preachers from the past? Is there any preacher (included here or not) who has impacted you personally? Who and why?
3. How has the presentation of biblical doctrine or teaching changed in the way sermons are delivered and executed today?

CHAPTER 2

Special Considerations for Preaching in the Twenty-First Century

Changes in the Way We Listen and How We Experience Church

I like to listen. I have learned a great deal from listening carefully. Most people never listen.

—ERNEST HEMINGWAY

Did you ever play a game called "telephone" or "gossip"? The point of the game is that a message is secretly shared by the first person in the group to a second person who then passes it on to the next person and so on. Each person passes on the message secretly as he or she understands it. Depending on the size of the group, it can get very interesting. Often what the first person actually said suffers a significant amount of change or distortion which tends to make the first person—the originator or first to pass on the message—wonder what could have happened to the original words. The point is that it is often a real challenge to "pass the message" as it was meant to be transmitted and received. Add to that the presumption in the preaching moment that people are actually listening and then comprehending the core of the message being presented, when we know that people can hear what they want to hear and understand what they choose to understand.

Preachers today are challenged by this reality. The fact is that those who listen to us each perceive a message that speaks to them, received and/or distorted through their own prejudices, concepts, theology, and attitudes about life and faith. Beyond those listening filters, the greatest challenges we face in preaching to contemporary audiences are yet to be discovered. There simply is not yet enough research to understand how listening works in the twenty-first century, especially as multi-tasking and decreasing attention spans are normative. To be focused on one thing, one message, one image, one sound is increasingly rare.

The challenges surrounding listening and comprehension, of course, have been before us for a very long time. While our focus in this work is church and not the classroom, when it comes to the present listening context and its challenges, there are important things to be learned from those involved in education, seeking ways to measure how their students (the listening audience) are either listening, attentive to what is being presented or distracted by other stimuli, prompted by access to a variety of new media.

In a study published in *Psychological Science* (Mueller and Oppenheimer)[1] two professors of psychology wanted to understand if note-taking with pen and paper was more effective for the learning process than using a laptop or notebook computer. In the study, students who used the longhand method performed better in answering questions on tests and appeared to have reinforced their understanding of the material.[2] Those who conducted the study were convinced their finding would be different. They had the impression that "heavy media multi-taskers" would be able to memorize, choosing what they paid attention to and what they were able to put aside. Yet their findings were the exact opposite. I would imagine the students who were heavy "multi-taskers" were also under the impression that they had a greater ability to retain information and be attentive than their colleagues who used wrote out their notes. However, that is clearly not the case.

---

1. Pam A. Mueller (Princeton) and Daniel E. Oppenheimer (University of California, Los Angeles), "The Pen Is Mightier Than the Keyboard: Advantages of Longhand Over Laptop Note Taking," *Psychological Science* 25 (June 2014): 1159-68 (citation continued on next page), accessed January 12, 2015, http://pss.sagepub.com/content/early/2014/04/22/0956797614524581.full.pdf+html.
2. Ibid.

A similar study at the University of Michigan Center for Research on Learning and Teaching (CRLT)[3] was aimed at helping students understand how using their computers in class could affect their attentiveness, engagement, and subsequent learning. One of the conclusions from this study appears to be more like a confession than an actual scientific conclusion. It turns out that 75% of the 595 students who participated in the study admitted that when they brought their laptops to the classroom, they used them for things such as email and chatting with friends on social media, a discovery that we can all be sure was not a great surprise to their professors.

What do studies on laptops in the classrooms and the use of other technology have to teach us about the way people in the pews listen to and receive the message preached in sermons? Is not the context totally different? Are not those people in the pews much more disconnected from the "outside world" when they come to church than those students in their large university classrooms? After more than two decades as a preacher, my conclusion is that there is a deep connection between those who sit in pews facing forward and young people sitting in a class room. This is especially so as our technology becomes more mobile; people are

---

3. Erping Zhu, Matthew Kaplan, R. Charles Dershimer and Inger Bergom, "Use Of Laptops in the Classroom: Research and Best Practices," *CRLT Occasional Papers* (University of Michigan, 2011), no. 30.

interacting simply by tapping their finger on a tiny screen. Laptop and larger computers are quickly becoming the secondary devices for daily and instant communication.

Furthermore, when the focus of attention is "up there" in the pulpit, the distance and barrier that the traditional pulpit represents may allow listeners to give their attention to other distractions. Perhaps this is a good reason for the preacher to make every effort to move around, standing closer to the people and avoiding a static position, as was often the norm in the past.

For years, I have heard members of congregations say, "Father, when the sermon is no good, I just read the church bulletin." Whether it is the laptop, the smart phone, the written page, there is always a way to disconnect and distract; we should be aware that those ways will continue to multiply.

For any communicator who takes those efforts seriously, some of the current research on listening, learning, and comprehension may be disconcerting. The words of Jesus as he explained to his disciples why he spoke in parables haunt us: ". . . they hear, but do not listen or understand."[4] While the evolution of social and other forms of media are impressive, the claim that we are somehow more connected than ever may be deceptive and far from the truth. In fact, one of the greatest challenges posed by new media is exactly that false impression of connectedness when we are truly

---

4. Matthew 13:13 (NIV)

disconnected from those who may be standing right in front of us.

Today's advances in science and technology allow neuroscientists to go inside the human brain, tracking its responses to a variety of stimuli, including the action of listening to the spoken word. This research is particularly interesting to the church, because in spite of new media and resources, most of us rely on the spoken word in a traditional format, without the aid of anything visual in our teaching and preaching.

Research confirms that the listening context—the way we listen and receive information—can stimulate totally different parts of our brains. We also know that the way in which a spoken message is delivered is closely linked to how effectively that message is received by the listener. We often speak of "listening to the sermon," yet we do not always make a distinction between the more casual act of hearing and actually perceiving and internalizing the spoken message. How much of what is preached today is ultimately understood in practical terms? The preached Word often calls for a response. But how is a response possible if the message has not been internalized or fully grasped? Diana Corley Schnapp has been a professor of communications for forty years, with an extensive background in religious studies. She writes,

A problem arises in writers' use of the word *listen* to mean *attention to and/or* responding to reading scripture or other religious writing in that if the written word is read, a different type of communication experience from listening occurs, and this calls for differing communication skills . . . . Unless the scripture

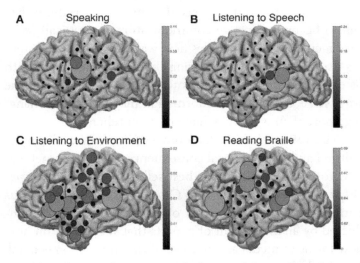

*Figure 1: Changes that occur in the brain while speaking, listening to speech, listening to the environment, and when reading Braille.**

*Jarod L. Roland, Carl D. Hacker, Jonathan D. Breshears, Charles M. Gaona, R. Edward Hogan, Harold Burton, Maurizio Corbetta and Eric C. Leuthardt, "Brain Mapping," *Frontiers in Human Neuroscience*, accessed October 5, 2014, http://journal.frontiersin.org/article/10.3389/fnhum.2013.00431/full 31 July 2013.

or religious experience is presented orally, is it accurate
to say that the receiver "listens to the Word?"[5]

Taking a closer look at some of the latest research
regarding the explosion of the use of social media among
children, youth, and adults makes clear why preachers must
not just become aware of the growing impact of new forms
of media on the craft of preaching, but do everything they
can to become effective communicators in a radically new
media culture. This includes new ways in which our listeners use their brains, recognizing that the dynamics of both
listening and speaking must now evolve. Our brains and the
way we receive and use information may indeed be changing, more than we can imagine or comprehend.

The author Nicholas Carr has written extensively on the
cultural and technological consequences of the internet and
new forms of media. In his best-selling book *The Shallows:
What the Internet Is Doing to Our Brains*, Carr presents us
with an enormous collection of studies and research conducted by an assortment of experts that sheds light on how
new forms of media and our use of the Internet, in general,
is indeed changing our way of reading, listening, comprehending, and retaining the information we receive. In his
chapter entitled "The Juggler's Brain" Carr states,

5. Diana Corley Schnapp, "Listening in Spirituality and Religion," in
Listening and Human Communication in the 21st Century ed. Andrew
D. Wolvin (Malden, MA: Blackwell Publishing, 2010), 246.

One thing is very clear: if, knowing what we know today about the brain's plasticity, you were to set out to invent a medium that would rewire our mental circuits as quickly and thoroughly as possible, you would probably end up designing something that looks and works a lot like the Internet. It's not just that we tend to use the Net regularly, even obsessively. It's that the Net delivers precisely the kind of sensory and cognitive stimuli—repetitive, intensive, interactive, addictive— that have been shown to result in strong and rapid alterations in brain circuits and functions . . . the Net may well be the single most powerful mind-altering technology that has ever come into general use.[6]

It is clearly evident that the use of Internet and new media indeed alters our brains and must, consequently, have some impact on the way we listen to sermons and any other form of the spoken word.

The latest investigations indicate that one in four persons living on the planet is now actively and regularly using social media. That is almost two billion people in the year 2015.[7] And there is little doubt that social media and other new forms of interactive media are changing the way we obtain and share information about almost every aspect of

6. Nicholas Carr, *The Shallows: What the Internet Is Doing to Our Brains* (New York: W.W. Norton and Company, 2011), 116.
7. Social Networking Fact Sheet, accessed November 20, 2014, http://www.pewinternet.org/fact-sheets/social-networking-fact-sheet/.

our lives, from looking for the right restaurant to choosing a house of worship to visit next weekend.

As part of my research for this book, I asked one hundred preachers and one hundred listeners of sermons to think with me about this new reality and the changes it was making in their preaching and their listening to sermons. The preachers came from various religious traditions, including two rabbis and a significant number of Anglican/Episcopal clergy throughout the United States, Canada, the Caribbean, and Latin America. It was my deliberate intention to engage those serving in a wide range of settings.

While this is a very small sampling of the influence of new forms of media among preachers and listeners, it is telling. What initially surprised me was the lack of significant disparity in most of the responses from both the preachers and from those who regularly listen to sermons. In both instances, almost three-quarters claimed new media has "some impact" to almost "no impact" in the way they preach or receive the message of sermons. The only discernible disparity found between lay people and clergy is that over ten percent more of the laity admitted to being influenced and/or affected by new media in the way they listen than the clergy acknowledged in the ways in which they preach.

Only two mega-church pastors and one Anglican priest who works with a younger demographic rated the impact at "10"; in other words they felt that new forms of media

Table 1: Survey Results

Questions	Some or no impact (1–5)	Significant impact (6–0)
PREACHERS (n=77)		
In your perception as a preacher, how do new forms of media (i.e. Internet, social media, mobile phones, tablets, etc.) impact your listeners and the listening context?	65 (84.42%)	12 (15.58%)
In your delivery and preparation as a preacher, what impact do these new forms of media have on your content and approach to preaching?	73 (94.81%)	4 (5.19%)
In my personal experience as a preacher, I would say the overall impact new forms of media have on my preaching experience is?	68 (88.31%)	9 (11.69%)
CONGREGANTS (n=95)		
As a congregant and listener of sermons, how and to what extent do new forms of media (i.e. Internet, social media, mobile phones, tablets, etc.) impact the way you listen to a sermon?	70 (73.68%)	25 (26.32%)
As an active listener of sermons, what impact do you perceive these new forms of media have on your preacher's approach to the craft of preaching?	90 (94.74%)	5 (5.26%)
In my personal experience, as a regular listener of sermons, I would say the overall impact new forms of media have on the way I listen to and receive sermons	80 (84.21%)	15 (15.79%)

have a huge or a very significant impact on them in their
task as preachers. Perhaps it is no surprise that these three
preachers have also experienced significant growth in their
congregations and are attracting young people in great
numbers.

We are now obliged to take another twist, which I
believe to be inspired and directly provoked by the evolution of new media and continued changes in the listening
context itself. It has to do with a radical departure from how
we traditionally understand the entire concept of church
itself, with preaching and traditional liturgy being at the very
core of that understanding. I am referring to the influence of
a younger generation of Christians today—within and even
outside the Emerging Church movements—and how they
perceive the effectiveness of traditional preaching and worship in general. Their claims are real and based on the fact
that we have a growing population of those who do not step
in the door to worship or hear a sermon. While most church
professionals do not appear to be overly interested in their
claims or approach, their message does clearly address the
issue of connecting people with the message of the Gospel,
a task at the very core of the mission entrusted to us by Jesus
himself to go out and spread good news.

While this movement has many names and faces and
is wide-ranging in its focus and theology, a young couple
from Perth, Western Australia, perhaps best illustrates the
power and motivation of this ecclesiological phenomenon

to move away from the traditional format of church into a new model of communication, resulting in a truly interactive church. Pastor Kevin-Neil Ward left his job as a successful pastor and church planter to join his wife Kathleen in trying to model what they understand to be closer to the early church and the experience of worship and faith lived out by the early Christian communities. They write,

> This century, the world around us is changing. The internet is the first ever truly two-way media. Instead of sitting back and being broadcasted at, we are now active participants and contributors. We now place a priority on connection, on being part of the conversation, on participation. People have 24/7 access to high-quality information and inspiration, so they no longer need to go to church for those things. Slowly but surely, these global, societal shifts are changing the way we do church . . . . More and more people in churches are tired of sitting silently, staring at the backs of each other's heads—they want to connect with one another, to love and support and encourage and build one another up, like the Bible tells us to. People are tired of meeting in special buildings and hiding away from the world around them—they want to transform their neighborhoods and communities. God's people are tired of being passive consumers, sitting back in the pews and quietly listening—they want to be active

participants, empowered to have a voice and make a difference.[8]

If we take a good look at this claim, much is being said about a new way of listening—and a new way of preaching. How is today's church responding to the huge paradigm shift occurring around us? This change, not limited to spoken language and the listening context, pertains specifically to the preaching most people hear and experience in thousands of houses of worship each weekend.

Social media and the Internet are also shaping the image of our churches even before people walk into them. Individuals and families looking for a place of worship may visit websites before deciding to attend in order to learn more about the parish, their ministries, location on the liberal-conservative spectrum, offerings for various age groups, etc. That discovery will mostly likely also include following links to learn more about the pastoral staff, listening or reading any sermons posted. The original sense of a "parish" as the area surrounding a church's building has been lost as visitors and members drive past several churches on the way to the one that best meets their perceived needs. Churches today are becoming more like restaurants: people

---

8. Kathleen and Kevin-Neil Ward, "How the Pulpit Is Changing in the 21st Century and Why It Is a Good Thing," accessed December 1, 2014, http://www.sermoncentral.com/pastors-preaching-articles /kathleen-and-kevin-neil-ward-how-the-pulpit-is-changing-in-the -21st-century-and-why-its-a-good-thing-2033.asp.

want to know what is being served there and what reviews they are getting before they consider visiting. The menu and offerings are carefully analyzed, and one significant item on that menu is the type of sermon, music, and overall worship made available. If visitors like the experience, they may rate your parish favorably, but if your sermon is boring, the incense is overwhelming, or your ushers are rude, you could get blacklisted in the world of social media.

One other challenge facing today's preachers is the fact that we are no longer preaching in a traditional Judeo-Christian society. Call it post-modern, neo-pagan, pluralistic, secular—whatever you choose to call it, it is becoming increasingly clear that we are no longer speaking to an audience that possesses a basic understanding of religious content or religious culture. Those "Happy Days" are gone, if they ever existed. Professor Stephen Prothero from the University of Boston has written several best-selling books on the matter.[9] In a recent presentation to journalists sponsored by the Pew Forum Religion and Public Life Project, Prothero spoke in his familiar humorous style and said,

> . . . most Americans cannot name any of the Gospels. It's about 50 percent, a little below, when you ask them to name a Gospel. Most don't know that Genesis is the first book of the Hebrew Bible. Ten percent think that Joan of Arc was Noah's wife. A sizeable minority

---

9. *Religious Literacy, God Is Not One, American Jesus* and others.

think that Sodom and Gomorrah were a happily married biblical couple. This is the kind of stuff you get when you ask about the Bible, you ask about Judaism and Christianity.[10]

The American Bible Society has commissioned surveys to measure the impact that the Bible has actually had in the life of individuals in the United States and throughout the world. One of their recent surveys revealed that while many people own Bibles and seem to think they know a lot about the biblical message, there is actually a huge disparity between owning a Bible and reading or studying it regularly: as many as forty-three percent of those surveyed were not able to name the first five books of the Bible.[11] The fact is that we cannot assume that the people we are preaching to or trying to engage in our churches have even the most basic biblical knowledge.

It is important, then, to be aware that this multi-tasking, technologically sophisticated audience may very well be in the dark ages when it comes to basic religious and theological concepts. In this sense, the listening context is not only impaired by outside stimuli and distractions, but by the very

---

10. Stephen Prothero, "Religious Literacy: What Every American Should Know" (Pew Forum Faith Angle Conference), accessed November 27, 2014, http://www.pewforum.org/2007/12/03/religious -literacy-what-every-american-should-know/.

11. Cathy Lynn Grossman, "Bible Survey: Many Americans Scramble Their Scripture," accessed November 28, 2014, http://www.religion news.com/2014/04/24/bible-women-war-american-bible-society-pew/.

fact that there is not a common foundation of biblical or religious understanding. This poses yet another challenge which preachers cannot ignore. In some ways, this sociological reality of the growing number of folks uninterested in religious and biblical matters is reminiscent of a humorous self-help relationship book written in 2009 entitled, *He's Just Not That Into You*, which was supposed to offer single women great advice on how to deal with issues in their romantic relationships. Perhaps it is time for us to have a version of this book for preachers, *They're Just Not That Into You*, referring to a congregation sitting in front of us each Sunday who may be connected to countless other things, but mostly not so interested in what we have to say. The challenges for today's preachers to make the biblical message relevant and applicable and to get the Gospel across effectively are indeed great!

Study Questions

1. How has the evolution of the listening context impacted the way we receive and transmit information?
2. Name three things that you believe have influenced your own way of listening in the present-day context and media culture.
3. How does an audience impact the craft of preaching and the content of a sermon? Must sermons adapt to the audience or the audience to the preacher—or message preached?

CHAPTER 3

How Approach, Style, and Delivery Influence the Reception of the Message

There are no uninteresting things, only uninterested people.
—G. K. CHESTERTON

Real estate experts often use the well-known mantra: "Location, location, location!" I wonder what preachers, liturgists, and theologians would use as a mantra to describe what they look for in a good sermon. Would it be content, delivery, or approach? For others, could it be exegesis, theology, or cohesion? Is there one word that could be turned into the essential preaching mantra? I wonder.

After looking at some aspects of the historical evolution of sermons and considering the particular challenges presented by twenty-first-century culture, I would like to suggest that a sermon has necessarily become a kind of "juggling act" demanding so much more from the preacher than was the case in the past. Today's preacher must indeed become a juggler: able to juggle the biblical message, grab the attention of an often-distracted congregation while maintaining a focused and organized train of thought, seek new anecdotes and stories that reflect the realities being lived today, know when to use humor and when to be more solemn, and, finally, connect it all in a way that comes across clearly to those receiving the Word preached.

As I see it, this juggling act is simply part of delivering the message to the brains of multi-taskers, people who are constantly stimulated—some would say over stimulated— by images, messages and external noise of every kind. Neither can one expect contemporary congregations to comprehend and engage a sermon that uses the same techniques that may have very effectively caught the imaginations of congregations in the past. Today, the preacher's ability to successfully keep that juggling act going is as important as the theological or spiritual content of the message itself. Our methods, expressions, and approaches to preaching must continue to evolve in order to connect with our ever-changing world.

It would be fair to say that perhaps we will never really be able to use one word to summarize good preaching or make it truly efficacious for listeners today. This is perhaps one of our greatest challenges as communicators of the Gospel. Are we able to pinpoint what we need to be doing in order to effectively communicate the Word? Beyond that, will we be able to form new preachers of the Gospel who are able to integrate sound theological principles with the tools of communication necessary to speak effectively today?

Seminaries have a long history of teaching two or three preaching classes while the candidates are in a residential program, yet very few seminaries offer even a single course in public speaking and effective communication. Theology and biblical principles are certainly a priority, but we live in a time when the tools for effective communication have become a basic requirement for almost every professional's life, regardless of their field of competence. We are preparing future communicators of the Gospel, yet we are not investing in their future as professional communicators: a sin of omission. In less theological terms, it is a serious deficiency in the formation of men and women who are going to be asked to be public speakers for the rest of their lives.

The research is clear that there are a growing number of young Americans who are indifferent toward the practice of faith or church affiliation. This is just one indicator that to a great number of young people in our society, the church has become boring, distant, or uninteresting. I suspect we could go further and say that they perceive that most of us church professionals and religiously affiliated adults are totally uninterested in them and in their issues. And in some cases, we have demonstrated just that, by putting ourselves an arm's distance away from our youth with an attitude that is often judgmental and not very welcoming.

It is not just young people who are feeling uninterested. It is no secret that most mainstream denominations continue to report steady declines in membership—a scary reality for many faithful believers, but fear will not resolve the issue. The fact is that preaching is at the very heart of the church's life and worship. A homily, both in its content and its delivery, must appeal, captivating those who listen to consider its message for their life. I believe the trends we see with young people are a reflection of what has been going on spiritually and religiously with their own parents and in their home lives. This disconnect does not occur in a vacuum; it is the result of years of inconsistent church affiliation and an inherited sense that the church is just "not that important" anymore. I believe it became unimportant when it became "uninteresting." In other words, the new question, as with so many other areas of contemporary society is "What is in it for me?" or even more specifically "How will the preaching I hear in my church make me a more spiritual person?" There is no doubt in my mind that the quality, approach and style of the sermon is certainly at the core of what could be, at least, part of the answer.

The Barna Group does extensive research in the area of religious trends in the United States. They have studied the issue of why Christians become "dropouts," "underchurched," "dechurched," or "unchurched." While some of this terminology may seem new to us, it certainly very clearly describes the phenomenon taking place around us. In one of their most recent studies on church attendance, we find truly astonishing and challenging figures:

As of 2014, the estimated number of people in the U.S. who Barna Group would define as "churchless"—meaning they have not attended a Christian church service, other than a special event such as a wedding or a funeral, at any time during the past six months—stands at 114 million. Add to that the roughly 42 million children and teenagers who are unchurched and you have 156 million U.S. residents who are not engaged with a Christian church. To put that in context, if all those unchurched people were a separate nation, it would be the eighth most populous country in the world, trailing only China, India, Indonesia, Brazil, Pakistan, Bangladesh, and the remaining churched public of the United States (159 million). In the past decade . . . the number of adults who are unchurched has increased by more than 30%. This is an increase of 38 million individuals—that's more people than live in Canada or Australia. The vast majority of America's churchless have attended a church. Very few of America's unchurched adults are purely unchurched—most of them, rather, are de-churched. Only about one-quarter of unchurched adults (23%) has never attended a Christian church at any time in his or her life, other than for a special service such as a wedding or funeral ceremony (though this number is on the rise; in 1993, only 15% of unchurched adults had never been connected to a church). The majority of unchurched individuals (76%) have first-hand experience with one or more Christian churches and, based on that sampling, have decided they can better use their time in other ways.[1]

Some may argue that these "dropouts" or "dechurched" folks are precisely not those to whom we are preaching, but I would venture to say that this could be a mistaken assumption on our part. Most of our congregations will get a handful of those folks who at some point got tired or became uninterested in church, but still come by casually and may drop in just to give it another try. Frequently they will come with mom or grandma, especially when they are visiting from out of town, and what we do at this crucial moment or how welcome they are made to feel may be just the thing that will bring them back. A well prepared and well executed sermon is critical to the well prepared space we make for those visitors, regardless of what brought them through the doors.

In my own diaconal and priestly ministry, I have often encountered those who felt the church had little or nothing to say to them. When they decide to give the church another try, it is usually due to a personal connection with a member

1. Barna Group, "10 Facts about America's Churchless," accessed December 10, 2014, https://www.barna.org/barna-update/culture/698 -10-facts-about-america-s churchless#.VLWGxrA3McA.

of the congregation who invites them to "hear my pastor." In my experience, a one time visitor most often becomes a regular attendee as a direct result of a positive experience with the sermon, with music and worship coming as later considerations. They are there for a sermon that will help them get through the week with an uplifting, biblical, and practical message. I find in my conversations with young adults in our parish and the greater community that more and more what is attracting people to attend any church on a regular basis is a sermon that speaks to them and motivates them to continue to live the Christian life. I have heard it time and time again in my twenty-plus years preaching, "Father, that sermon really hit home." It appears that more people today are choosing churches because they feel they are "being fed" or receiving direct spiritual guidance and support from the preaching event, which typically occurs during the Sunday service. Denominational fidelity to the church of their upbringing is not a very big motivator any more. Could this be why so many of the mega-churches use a "self-help" approach to their preaching? Are there any lessons there for those of us who are not in the mega-church movement?

In 2001, when I began to write my syndicated newspaper columns, *El Nuevo Herald* (the *Miami Herald*'s Spanish-language paper), I worked with a fine Editor-in-Chief who had been a newspaper man most of his life. Mr. Carlos Castañeda's greatest concern each and every day—and perhaps the single greatest reason he was such a successful editor—was the content and layout of the front page of the next day's paper. He always said that what went on the front page of the newspaper was like "dressing up the monkey," attracting people to pick it up, buy it, and read it.

Likewise, there are four aspects of preaching which have nothing to do with theological aptitude, hermeneutics, biblical knowledge, or the more academic aspects of an effective sermon, which while totally necessary, may not be what will attract most people to the message being delivered. Let us focus on these four things that will help us to "dress the monkey" in order to attract listeners to this very important message: *know the audience, use humor and anecdotes, know where to stand, and avoid reading from a written text.*

Know the Audience

As early as the sixth century, Gregory the Great, shortly after his election as Bishop of Rome, wrote *The Book of Pastoral Rule* in which he emphasized the preacher's role in getting to know the audience and adapting the sermon to the particular needs of the listeners. He often referred to homiletics as "the art of preaching" and was known to be an extremely eloquent preacher himself. When speaking on the importance of this connection with the congregation, Gregory said,

> For the things that profit some often hurt others; seeing that also for the most part herbs which nourish some animals are fatal to others; and the gentle hissing that

quiets horses incites whelps; and the medicine which abates one disease aggravates another; and the bread which invigorates the life of the strong kills little children. Therefore according to the quality of the hearers ought the discourse of teachers to be fashioned, so as to suit all and each for their several needs, and yet never deviate from the art of common edification. For what are the intent minds of hearers but, so to speak, a kind of tight tensions of strings in a harp, which the skillful player, that he may produce a tune not at variance with itself, strikes variously?[2]

If anyone ever tells you that preaching the Gospel is exactly the same in every context and congregation, I can assure you that person is seriously lacking pastoral experience. Even if a church offers a variety of services at different times, provides different lengths of the service, and caters to diverse populations, the sermon must be addressed to the particular crowd and must address the needs of those present. It is not an identical experience to preach to a group of senior citizens as to a church full of children, youth, and families. Likewise, congregations include people of a variety of socio-economic backgrounds, which could require special

---

2. Gregory the Great, *The Book of Pastoral Rule*, part III, 1-3, translated by James Barmby, *A Select Library of Nicene and Post-Nicene Fathers of the Christian Church*, vol. XII (New York: The Christian Literature Company, 1894), 25.

care. Knowing the congregation is a significant part of effective communication and effective preaching.

It is also important to recognize the faith traditions, customs, and practices of your particular congregation. In Anglicanism, for instance, where there are a variety of liturgical and theological inclinations (i.e., Anglo-Catholic, Evangelical, Low Church, Broad Church, etc.) preaching can take a different level of significance depending on the congregation's particular bent. While the Gospel carries a strong message of justice, equity, and reconciliation, the pulpit is not a place to air one's political or social agenda, but a sacred space for proclaiming the good news of Jesus Christ. Whenever a clergy person turns the pulpit into their own platform, they are forgetting that those precious moments belong to the Lord and his people; it is intended to be a time for edification and renewal. When we know our congregation and truly care for their needs and not our own, we get out of the way and the Word will be proclaimed.

Use Humor and Anecdotes

The use of humor in sermons varies from very good to very bad, with only a few landing in between. Humor in sermons is far more than joke-telling, and preachers must be aware that humor or any other instrument we use to connect with the audience must not be confused for a gimmick or something superficial. Experience has taught me that humor connects like very few other things can. The effective preacher must first seek to be an effective communicator, storyteller, and master at proclamation of the Word. The preacher is a presenter of lively images that are integrated into the message to make it come alive for the listeners. To tell a joke disconnected from anything that will follow and then start a sermon is a useless exercise and will not help you or your listeners in any way. However, if you integrate your humor (or anecdote or inspirational story) as part of your message, you create the types of connectors in people's minds that will keep the message of the sermon alive for them. If it is done well, it can be like the gravy on your turkey dinner: it just makes an already good thing better. Good images, stories, and humor are all at the service of making the power of God's message in the sermon more digestible and easier to comprehend.

Joseph Webb has a multi-faceted background applying his knowledge of media and journalism to the craft of Christian preaching. He is the author of several books on preaching and communications. In his work, *Comedy and Preaching*, he makes an argument against those who would dismiss the use of comedy and anecdotes in preaching as something that devalues preaching or takes away from its integrity. He emphasizes the very point which is being made in this chapter:

> In a recent meeting of the Academy of Homiletics, the annual gathering of men and women who teach preaching in seminaries, no less a homiletician than Henry Mitchell, the great African American scholar, presented

a paper in which he discussed what he believes preaching is going to have to be to survive in the third millen-
nium. He said that is it necessary to clarify the meaning
of a couple of terms, one of which was entertainment.
"We say that we don't believe in religion as entertainment," Mitchell said. "We believe in preaching educational sermons, not entertaining ones. Well, the opposite
of entertaining is boring, not educational. And unless
we engage an audience, we need not try to teach them
anything at all. Our problem is simply how to entertain
with integrity, how to engage an audience compellingly,
with the gospel, and for high purposes [his emphases]."
What Mitchell expressed is that it is time to quit putting down sermons that entertain, as though they are
somehow not theological or even spiritual. It is time,
instead, to embrace the idea that the pulpit is a place
where something called entertainment not only can but
should go on. Boredom fostered by the pulpit not only
is not being tolerated by contemporary people, many of
whom are now former churchgoers, but it will not be
tolerated as a preaching paradigm of the future.[3]

I could not agree more. Boring and uninteresting are simply
not going to make it in the preaching of the twenty-first century. Today's audiences are certainly more demanding, have

---

3. Joseph M. Webb, *Comedy and Preaching* (St. Louis: Chalice Press,
1998), 38.

more access to media, and need the message presented in a more appealing and compelling way. Communications have changed and evolved. It is time for preaching to ride the wave of change if it is to be a relevant force in the present culture and listening context. Henry Mitchell's challenge is consistent with the data we are receiving on new trends in church attendance, or lack thereof. It is not a matter of confusing good and effective preaching with light theology or a watered-down Gospel, however it is important to deliver sermons that are accessible to people accustomed to a new form of communication in almost every other aspect of their lives. Why should a seminar at work feel appealing and inspiring, but a sermon at church feel like a chore to bear?

As one who has been a regular weekly—and sometimes daily—preacher in two mainstream Christian denominations for over twenty years, I have witnessed the significant pressure on preachers to create homilies that are biblical, smart, and contain theological and spiritual content for a congregation to chew on. Toward that goal, most preachers spend hours preparing their sermon, writing it out word for word each week. Yet, oftentimes, what is lost in these well prepared sermons are these connectors I keep insisting on. I am referring to all those details that have very little to do with the content of a sermon, yet are critical in getting that content to engage the congregation. Consider the icing on a cake. While the icing is not the main ingredient, nor is it the most substantial part of the treat, it makes the whole experience so different, so much more palatable. Maybe it is the equivalent of what my old newspaper friend described as "dressing the monkey."

There is an added benefit to this approach and style that cannot be overlooked. The preacher exposes his or her *humanity* in using anecdotes, and especially humor. The listener tends to feel much more connected to a preacher who can laugh, readily demonstrating that he or she can feel and express emotions as part of daily experience. Perhaps we no longer live in a time when we question the humanity of our clergy. Today's preachers must not limit themselves to preaching the incarnational Gospel of the Word Made Flesh, but they must also be human and accessible themselves— real people with real feelings. Too many of our intellectual preachers today boast of an "incarnational theology," but their preaching style does not in any way make it "flesh that dwells among us." It does not serve the church when clergy appear to be cold and distant, even if only in their speaking or preaching style. The more natural we are in our preaching voice and style, the greater our impact will be on our listeners. These are indeed new demands made by our new media culture, and they are impacting all communicators, including clergy

Avoid the Reading of a Written Text

There is a story told by Fulton J. Sheen of an old Irish lady who was hearing a bishop read a lengthy sermon, and in a moment of desperation, she said out loud: "Glory be to God, if he can't remember what he's saying, how does he expect us to?" If we understand that the pulpit can create a physical barrier, reading a sermon from a printed text can have a similar effect in that the reader may be looking down in order to read and flip pages while missing the opportunity for eye contact with his or her listeners. I realize that many people have grown accustomed to listening to sermons read and some preachers can only preach with a text, but it is an outdated habit that needs to be given up. Our culture demands that we look at ways of capturing the imaginations and the attention of twenty-first-century listeners. Only in very formal settings, such as a commencement speech or an address at the United Nations, do people read from a text today. In many cases, this happens when the language spoken is not the speaker's native tongue, or a language in which they are not fluent. While I understand this is difficult for many preachers to accept, they are indeed communicating in a style that is no longer "in style." Those who present the news, elected officials, and other public speakers who use a text almost exclusively use prompters today, precisely so that their remarks do not appear read. There is a reason for this—and it has to do with credibility and connectedness. Imagine someone reading the news cast from a printed text today, like it was done at the beginning of television. People probably would not watch. Yet, that is exactly how many individuals are taught to preach. We read. Someone looking down at a text, standing behind a pulpit, flipping pages and engaging us with limited amounts of eye contact is not serving the preaching event. I can't imagine our Lord, in the middle of the Sermon on the Mount saying to Peter and Andrew, "Can you guys please fetch my text; I forgot what comes next."

Preachers need to move away from the rehearsed, written text and teach themselves to speak from an organized outline that lends itself to greater spontaneity and a more effective and natural delivery. Even if we were to look at the origins of the read sermon, they are not so clear. Yet, David Larsen, in his book, *The Anatomy of Preaching: Identifying The Issues in Preaching Today*, says it started under Henry VIII in England, and he certainly has a few strong and well-defined opinions on the issue. He writes:

> The reading of the sermon manuscript actually originated during the reign of King Henry VIII of England. This is the most difficult and the least acceptable of the methods used in our day. The great problem with it is that it sounds written and read. The visual society in which we live has plunged us into a new communications ball game. The world of print must yield to the speech event . . . long before television it was realized that reading the sermon creates distance . . . . Paper is not a good conductor of heat . . . . Every break in eye contact is risky, especially when that break comes toward the end of the sentence and is often accompanied by a voice drop.[4]

---

4. David L. Larsen, *The Anatomy of Preaching: Identifying the Issues in Preaching Today* (Grand Rapids: Baker Book House, 1992), 187–88.

Perhaps we grew up in a parish with great preachers who were accustomed to using a written manuscript and we grew accustomed to that style of preaching. Maybe we are attached to the cerebral and more academic sermon that often requires us to write each word. Whatever the case may be, preachers who are committed to excellence must not forget that the art of good communication also evolves and, in order for that quality communication to occur more effectively in our present context, it will require that we too evolve. There is little room for the preacher's own preferences, fears, and attachments to habits formed in the past. On the contrary, the preacher today must be willing to accept the challenge of speaking and connecting with a radically new audience that will require a new methodology and approach—part of a listening context that is rapidly changing, as we observed in Chapter 2.

Michael J. Quicke, author of *360 Degree Preaching: Hearing, Speaking, and Living the Word*, puts it in context for us:

Preaching in the twenty-first century means preaching in the midst of change. Lyle Schaller describes three basic options when facing change: to sit back, to plunge in blindly, or to learn from experience so that an anticipatory style of leadership is developed. Some preachers in well-established congregations that are biblically literate and expect traditional preaching can sit back and claim that the effects of culture shift are overstated and that the old ways are the best. Other preachers seem to plunge too quickly into novelty. Instead, preachers need to develop an anticipatory style of leadership in which they learn, listen, and dare to preach afresh. One aspect of such leadership is a preacher's self-awareness of where he or she is in the range of preaching opportunities in the twenty-first century.[5]

For those who have a hard time with the change they experience within their congregations and in the society that surrounds them, I only have bad news: there is more of it on the way. On the other hand, for those looking for a challenge I say, "Hang on for the ride of your life because this communications boom is big enough and dynamic enough to take us in a variety of new and exciting directions." If it is happening in every other aspect of life and the society we live in, why would it not happen in church?

I am convinced that some of the new forms of media and the interactive opportunities they create are already very actively helping the church in its sacred mission to "preach the gospel to every creature."[6] The contemporary preacher of the good news must see an opportunity to build

---

5. Michael J. Quicke, *360 Degree Preaching: Hearing, Speaking and Living the Word* (Grand Rapids: Baker Academic, 2003), 110.
6. Mark 16:15 (NIV).

bridges where there may be huge gaps and to reach today's faithful in a language they can comprehend and that will lead to the type of transformation which only the message of Jesus can offer. Media is not our enemy, but a welcomed conduit to the mission of bringing good news to the world. It is true that more communication does not necessarily mean *better* or more effective communication, but the challenge we are presented with today is to constantly identify where media and the mission of Christ's Church meet and even mesh. Think about it: biblical scholars and students of the New Testament would have a lot less to do if there had been satellites or cable in Paul's time. Instead of twenty-seven books in the New Testament, we could have ended up with ten or so because the Corinthians, Thessalonians, Philippians and Romans all received the same letters. But seriously, today the Church is able to communicate with the whole world, not just with the congregations sitting in our pews. This presents us with a real challenge and an exciting possibility—one that we cannot pass up.

Study Questions

1. How do anecdotes and humor reinforce the connection with those listening to sermons and the focus it may provide for the message preached? Refer to good and bad experiences you have witnessed with the use of these tools.

2. To read or not to read . . . What are your thoughts on the preacher reading a manuscript every time he or she gets up to preach?

3. Do you perceive new communications styles as somehow helping the craft of preaching or are they taking away from it?

CHAPTER 4

How Liturgical Churches Can Preach Effective Contemporary Sermons

Don't say infinitely when you mean very;
otherwise you'll have no word left
when you want to talk about something really infinite.
—C. S. LEWIS

It is Sunday morning and the people are coming in to the church building from the parking lot. As one car stops, each family member takes a glance at their phone to see a post on Facebook or Instagram, read a tweet, or send a last minute text message or email. The mother can be heard instructing them all, including her husband, "Silence your phones, it's time for church." As they make their way into the beautiful nineteenth-century gothic structure which is their parish church, the youngest members of the family, firmly clenching their mobile devices, are greeted at the door by an usher who hands them a printed bulletin and a book from which to sing and pray.

I bring these realities to our attention not because I think every church needs to have touch screens in the narthex or big screens instead of hymnals, even though I realize a number of us do. Rather, I point to these realities because I am convinced that even the most traditional, liturgical, and ceremonial churches have the opportunity to preach imaginative, creative, and effective sermons that will build up the faith of those who hear them. It is precisely in the homiletical moment that we want people to be fully engaged with what is happening and least interested in reaching for that device in their pocket, even if it is just to check the time, date, or weather.

Communications Theory Meets Homiletics

There is a tendency to think that if we apply too much creativity to our preaching, using great stories, jokes, and images, there will not be time for serious biblical exegesis or an in-depth reflection on the readings for the day. This is simply not true. There is no reason why communication within the church (and to those outside our walls) cannot be enhanced and even rescued by the world of professional communications. As a matter of fact, I would say that this is an urgent integration needed in today's church, even though many clergy persons may not feel ready to accept it.

William Brosend, in *The Preaching of Jesus: Gospel Proclamation Then and Now* points out how preachers can indeed do both—be interesting and avoid being boring:

> Is it possible that the reason people are not very interested in our sermons is that our sermons are often not very interesting? I know that it is not feasible to be good every week, and I often point out that if we batted one for three every game, we would make the Hall of Fame. But is that an excuse to plan to be boring? Yet we are, week in and week out. We plan on being boring, sometimes because of the way we structure our sermons, beginning with our conclusion and hoping folks will hang on to the end anyway. More likely, we plan to be boring because we have planned our sermon preparation time to focus almost exclusively on exegesis, theological analysis, reflection, and shaping and developing our thoughts. We leave almost no time to shape and develop our words in order to bring our thoughts to life . . . it is more important to have something to say than to say it well; but *good* preaching is both.[1]

Rather than trying to fit it all in on Sunday, we may want to leave some of the exegetical and heavier teaching work for Bible study in the middle of the week and use more of our sermon time to answer the "fundamental homiletical

---

1. William Brosend, *The Preaching of Jesus: Gospel Proclamation Then and Now* (Louisville: Westminster John Knox, 2010), 134.

question," which according to Brosend is: "What does the
Holy Spirit want the People of God to hear from these texts
on this occasion?"[2] If preachers take the time to answer
that question as they begin sermon preparation, it is almost
impossible that the outcome is a boring sermon, because
we are counting on God speaking to his people through the
craft of preaching. I often say to the folks at the parishes that
I have served that I am just "an accident of the Holy Spirit."
At first, I see hesitation on some faces. But when I explain to
them that we are musical instruments capable of producing
sounds, but that God is the musician and the music, then
they get it. Hence, it is part of remembering that we preachers are at the service of God's message and not our own.

Much has been written on communication theory, the
theology of communication, and a host of other areas that
would serve the contemporary preacher's ongoing formation in becoming a more effective communicator. Yet very
few works are written with the style and appeal we find
in Charles H. Kraft, a noted pastor and long-time professor
of anthropology and communications at Fuller Theological
Seminary. Among his dozens of published works, there is
one I consider to be a little "jewel" that should be man-
datory reading for every seminarian and preacher of the
Gospel in our times: *Communication Theory for Christian
Witness*. While the latest revised edition was published in

2. Ibid., 48.

1991 (eighth printing), this work is perhaps one of the most complete Christian texts in the area of effective communication and offers a complete understanding of the art of communication as it relates to preaching and the church's mission in our world. Kraft breaks down some of the myths of communication and uses Jesus as a point of reference and example of good and effective communication. Kraft says,

> God's way is to use ordinary, highly communicative language to convey spiritual truth . . . . Truly effective communicators are more concerned with "preciseness" in the way people respond to their messages than with the preciseness of their vocabulary. They, therefore, prepare carefully but with a very different emphasis than those who aim at technical preciseness. *They concern themselves with personal factors more than with the impersonal, structural, and linguistic factors in message construction.* They are constantly conscious of and oriented toward the impression their messages make on their receptors.[3]

Kraft's challenge to preachers today is to be more intentional about the message and less concerned with what we think people need to hear. In other words, the sermon is not the time to give an exposition of how much you learned or how well you did in New Testament Studies

---

3. Charles H. Kraft, *Communication Theory for Christian Witness* (New York: Orbis Books, 1991), 33.

while in seminary, but a real opportunity for transformation in the lives of God's people through the preaching of God's Word. While I recognize this is difficult for many preachers to hear, since this is the time and place when they are able to reach the largest number of congregants, the preaching event on Sunday morning is not a substitute for Adult Education or an effective Bible Study program. More emphasis is needed on the listeners and less concern with the technicality of what the preacher may feel is of importance. This immediately turns our preaching into something more inspirational and practical than theological and technical. For the most part, people will also digest it and apply it more effectively.

My point is that communications theory and homiletics *should* meet, and they should meet often. Ultimately, one of our biggest problems comes down to this: many preachers are in a business they simply do not know well or have not truly been professionally prepared for. In most cases, we train seminarians in theology, filling their minds with great philosophical and theological concepts, yet they will be expected to stand up each Sunday and be professional orators; public speakers who can captivate and communicate a message we consider the most important message for all to hear. We spend little, if any, time helping future clergy to be excellent public speakers. They take two or three preaching classes and preach a few times in class and to a local congregation before being ordained to preach the Good News to the world. To form effective communicators, we must do much more to teach even basic communication skills to those we are expecting to speak professionally—and probably for the rest of their lives.

A Return to the Jesus Method

A return to what I call the "Jesus Method" which uses what Kraft describes as "ordinary, highly communicative language" could be precisely what the church needs most at this time. When we look at the Lord's use of the most simple language and earthly examples to convey a spiritual lesson, I often wonder what has happened to most of us who are his preachers. The Jesus Method is not often seen or heard on Sunday mornings. There is no stiffness, complicated-to-grasp theology or exegesis, or difficult ideas to connect and comprehend anywhere in the preaching of Jesus, but there is certainly a lot of that coming from our pulpits on Sunday mornings. Even when Jesus uses images that are difficult to grasp, he tends to explain them or to connect them with some reality that is clearly understood by his listeners.

The Sunday liturgy is full of ritual. This is right since the very nature of the liturgy requires a sense of structure and order. In The Episcopal Church we use The Book of Common Prayer as our guide for liturgy, although it does offer great flexibility within its pages. Recent studies confirm that people between eighteen and twenty years old (often referred to as "Millennials") are very much attracted to the traditional buildings for worship—and a worship style that focuses on silence and a sense of mystery—over the auditorium, warehouse-looking churches.[4]

So why are some young people attending these "warehouse churches" and driving right by their home parish in order to be fed spiritually? According to Thom Rainer, who has done extensive research in the area of reaching the "unchurched" or "unaffiliated," most people are attracted to the pastor and the preaching first.[5] It is mostly because of their expectations of a dynamic sermon that new people may even contemplate walking in. The reason so many of our mainstream denominations are declining so rapidly, is that there is a communication gap that has been created by a message that is not perceived as relevant to contemporary ears. We need to find new ways to connect the Word with those who come seeking it. You may think this is a matter of theology, but I am convinced it is mostly a matter of effective communications strategy.

---

4. "Designing Worship Spaces with Millennials in Mind" (November, 2014), accessed December 5, 2014, https://www.barna.org/barna-update/millennials/689-designing-worship-spaces-with-millennials-in-mind#.VLanjdLF_Db.

5. Rainer, Thom. *Surprising Insights from the Unchurched and Proven Ways to Reach Them* (Grand Rapids: Zondervan, 2008), 53.

Allowing Our Sermons and Ourselves to Be Evaluated

Bill Hybels is the pastor of one of the largest churches in the world. He started out as a youth minister in the 1970s doing what most preachers of the time did: conversational, dialogue preaching.[6] Yet, he realized that he continued to have the same twenty-five youth each week and they were not very interested in what he was preparing for them. It was not until he began to perceive the real needs of his listeners and tried to connect with those needs that he was able to preach and teach those young people. He claims the strength of his preaching comes from being evaluated by folks in his congregation, something that makes most clergy cringe. Yet Hybels is convinced that his success as preacher began with implementing the practice of honest and regular evaluation. He says, "Every preacher is evaluated, one way or another, by every listener. Constructive evaluation won't happen, though, no matter how willing I am to receive it, unless I am asking the right people the right questions at the right time."[7]

Rather than being evaluated superficially at the door as people leave the church, shake hands, and murmur "great

---

6. Bill Hybels, Stuart Briscoe, and Haddon Robinson, *Mastering Contemporary Preaching* (Portland, OR: Christianity Today, 1989), 153.

7. Hybels, et al, *Mastering Contemporary Preaching*, 153.

sermon," could this become something that empowers members of the congregation to think about the sermon and evaluate its value in their lives? Can the result of this type of evaluation be not only better preaching but a congregation more engaged with the sermon itself? Perhaps this kind of two-way engagement would help close whatever gap may exist between preacher and congregation. In the appendix of his book, *Preaching and Leading Worship*, one of the greatest preachers in the English language, Will Willimon, offers a very practical form of evaluation entitled, "Sermon Reaction Questionnaire."[8] This interesting survey can be easily filled out by anyone in the congregation because of its simplicity and directness. It targets everything from eye contact to content and even allows the listeners to evaluate if the sermon went on "too long." Sensitive pastors and preachers should beware, because the questionnaire is written in the style typical of someone who is known for being direct.

Willimon also makes a strong connection between the importance of personal integrity and an authentic spiritual life. Do we preachers realize that our lives may be in for much tougher evaluation than our words ever will be? As a bishop in the United Methodist Church and long-time professor with an extensive history of training future ministers of the gospel, Willimon knows better than most what it takes

---

8. Will H. Willimon, *Preaching and Leading Worship* (Philadelphia: The Westminster Press, 1984), appendix.

to preach a good sermon and what makes good preachers, really good ones. He observes:

> Homiletical habits—disciplines, weekly study, honesty and humility about what the text says and does not say, confidence in the ability of God to make our puny congregations worthy to hear God's Word, a weekly willingness to allow the Word to devastate the preacher before it lays a hand on the congregation—all these are habits, skills of the homiletical craft, which form us preachers into better people than we would be if we had been left to our own devices.[9]

The good preacher becomes a good sermon! The people of God are seeking living sermons: stories of faith and courage, of healing and reconciliation, of strength and true discipleship, of brokenness restored. Willimon's point can be scary; whether we choose to be aware of it or not, we become living sermons in the flesh. Our faith is incarnational and people are also seeking incarnate models of faith. The Word became flesh and the Word also becomes flesh through the witness of the preacher's Christian living, which is perhaps the best sermon we can all preach. Thus, the famous quote attributed to St. Francis of Assisi when questioned by his followers why they were not preaching more aggressively

---

9. Will H. Willimon, "The Preacher as an Extension of the Preaching Moment," in *Preaching on the Brink: The Future of Preaching*, ed. Martha J. Simmons (Nashville, TN: Abingdon Press, 1996), 169.

on the streets. Popular legend has it that the young Francis responded by saying, "Preach the Gospel at all times. If necessary, use words." Willimon's perspective is that every aspect of a preacher is evaluated as an integral part of the preaching experience.

Most theological schools, bible colleges, and seminaries offer opportunities through homiletics and preaching courses for their students to focus on the strengths and weaknesses of their preaching and that of their colleagues. This can cause tension among students and even a sense of competition. After the seminarian graduates and is ordained for ministry, often beginning a steady dose of preaching and teaching, what now? Will he or she continue to receive feedback on their sermons? Appendix III in this book offers a simple and effective method of evaluation which can be done at the parish level regularly, inviting congregational evaluation. This can be completed anonymously with the form being given to various members of the congregation by ushers or greeters. No more than seven to ten people should be asked to participate at once; otherwise it becomes too obvious and can be distracting. At the end of the sermon the person inserts the small form inside a provided envelope marked SERMON. The participant seals it and drops it in the offering basket. Those who count the offering set aside the evaluations for the preacher to read on Monday morning. Since only the preacher will see the results, this offers the evaluator greater freedom to express him or herself. This process can be done quarterly, but perhaps, some may find it useful to do it with greater frequency. Whatever the case, the preacher must not fall into the trap of modeling his sermon solely based on preferences or comments. The feedback is not dogma—it is just feedback. Having time to discern and discover what those evaluations mean will be just as vital to the evaluation process.

Study Questions

1. How important is it for a preacher of the Gospel to be an effective communicator? Are seminary programs spending enough time teaching students to be effective and dynamic public speakers?
2. Do you sense that contemporary preachers are willing and ready to be evaluated by their colleagues and congregations? Have you ever been involved in the evaluation of a sermon? Describe what that experience was like.

CHAPTER 5

Sermons That Connect with the Twenty-First-Century Listener

*Too many church services start at eleven sharp
and end at twelve dull.*

—VANCE HAVNER

It seems that every aspect of life is *reviewed* today. That is increasingly becoming part of living in the midst of our interactive culture, especially with our multiple social media outlets, inviting us to like, share, comment, and review almost everything, instantly. For example, if someone goes to a restaurant and the service or food is not good, they can easily use their phones to find a myriad of folks who agree. It is truly fascinating to see how much the evaluation of others—even those we do not know—is becoming a part of the way we make decisions. It is no different when it comes to church and especially when it comes to preaching. Whether or not we are ready to accept it, most people are looking for the kind of preaching and church experience that offers them something spiritual they can take home with them. Your sermon may be eloquent, highly exegetical, and even theologically deep, but if it does nothing to connect the message of sacred scripture in some practical way for the people in the congregation, your sermon did not achieve its purpose to proclaim the Good News.

A Sermon That *Did Not* Connect at All

I had the privilege of being invited by the Presiding Bishop of The Episcopal Church to preach at a special bilingual Eucharist at the 77th General Convention in July, 2012.[1] As one who has been preaching regularly for twenty years, it should not have been a nerve-racking experience, but it was. Here I was, a somewhat new Episcopalian, being granted a privilege that many of my colleagues have never had. It was a big deal! Then came the memo saying I was to preach between seven to ten minutes, it had to be written out for the official church website, and it had to be in English and

---

1. The Rev. Albert R. Cutie, "On the Feast of Bartolome de las Casas," sermon at the 77th General Convention of the Episcopal Church, Indianapolis, Indiana, July 2012, accessed February 25, 2015, https://episcopalchurch.wistia.com/medias/6ynzmhvsva.

Spanish. The English and Spanish wasn't a problem, but ten minutes? Written text? Really? The last time I had written out a full sermon, word for word, was as a twenty-four year old seminarian, completing my Master of Divinity degree, for an assignment in our preaching class.

I have never been an anxious or nervous preacher, but to be asked to preach for an assembly like this, with the Presiding Bishop, my own bishop, and a host of other church leaders staring up at me from the front row expecting to hear a great sermon, was very different from the norm. It was not my typical Sunday crowd—my comfort zone; it was as uncomfortable as it gets. The more I analyzed it, the more I realized my biggest concern was that I did not preach well from a prepared text. I always mentally prepared my text and outline, but I did not read a manuscript as I preach; it was not fluid for me, and I sensed an immediate barrier between me and the audience.

Michael Rogness has been a Lutheran pastor and seminary professor of homiletics at Luther Seminary in St. Paul, Minnesota. In his work, *Preaching to a TV Generation*, he says:

> In the past, when the sermon manuscript lay completed on the desk, the pastor could sit back and say with satisfaction, "Finally, it's done!" All that remained was to read it to the congregation. That is no longer true. With a completed manuscript we are half done. Now we have to learn it. A good sermon has to be well written and well delivered. In the age of television,

> many a fine sermon dies from poor delivery . . . . The
> age of reading before an audience is gone![2]

Perhaps what I experienced reading that sermon is part of what Rogness is referring to.

Can it be that we are just not hard-wired for read messages anymore? Is it possible that the church, by accepting sermons read from a manuscript, is insisting on using a communications tool that, like the telegram or an old manual typewriter, is no longer effective? Is it possible that even Rogness's twenty-year old book is now outdated and that the problem is no longer the TV generation, but the here-comes-every-form-of-media-possible generation? I believe so. I am certain that the challenge is even much greater today, in the post-television generation.

As I look back, I am convinced that preaching from a text is what mostly killed my convention sermon, for a variety of reasons. By its very nature, a bilingual sermon must be something somewhat spontaneous. It requires one to go back and forth between languages often, keeping in mind that the audience which understands one language and not the other is waiting, perhaps impatiently, for you to resume in the language they comprehend. It is a tricky exercise, but it can be done well with some practice. For some reason, when I was told I had to write a manuscript, I lost the dynamism

---

2. Michael Rogness, *Preaching to a TV Generation: The Sermon in the Electronic Age* (Lima, OH: CSS Publishing, 1994), 94–95.

of the "back and forth" which I would normally have had in a bilingual sermon. At times, it can even be humorous for both audiences, the English speakers and Spanish speakers, because they sense that there are so many Anglicized words in our contemporary use of Spanish that translation of certain things will easily make some folks laugh. And we cannot deny that this element of participation and active listening is certainly part of an effective sermon when the listeners are truly into it. Whether you are speaking in English or in Spanish, the fact remains that effective communicators engage their listeners. The language spoken is simply a matter of circumstance, yet the level of enthusiasm and engagement that we must bring to the craft of preaching is never accidental. It must be deliberate, and the preacher needs to be aware of it before he or she stands up to preach.

Now that I have spent quite a bit of time insisting that contemporary preachers move away from the written text—and hopefully—from behind the pulpit, I must say that some very talented preachers do very well in their use of a prepared text and have demonstrated the ability to make it a truly dynamic and engaging experience. If this works for them and their preaching tone is not becoming monotonous because they are so strongly tied to their written manuscript, then by all means they should use it. But, in all fairness, experience has shown me that highly effective manuscript preachers are in the minority. Reading or preaching from the written text requires a certain kind of art that few public speakers have. Even the simple exercise involved in flipping pages and keeping track of where they left off, while at the same time trying to maintain some sort of eye contact with the congregation is often a challenge not met and can become a huge distraction. I am convinced this kind of preaching and method of public speaking belongs to ages past and the more we listen to contemporary communications experts challenging us to use more extemporaneous speaking and move away from manuscript reading, the better our preaching will be for today's listener. Ultimately, the challenge is to connect with the congregation.

Why Preachers Connect or Disconnect

Many things can go wrong with sermons. Sometimes, they just start on the wrong foot and never quite recuperate. It's my sense that if I don't grab the congregation in the first two or three minutes, it is probably not going to be a good or effective sermon. It has been my experience that when a preacher does not make a deliberate effort to connect with listeners from the beginning, the congregation is given the opportunity to find something else they will connect with and focus on, whether that is reading the announcements in the bulletin or discovering details in the stained glass window they had never noticed before.

An effective preacher cannot begin a sermon by saying, "I know you just heard this great passage of scripture, and I will get to it eventually, but I am first going to talk to you about something else I have on my mind." In the craft of preaching, we are facilitators of the Holy Spirit, and we must be mindful of the fact that it is God's Spirit which is seeking to speak to God's people. A preacher should never decide there is something more pressing than the Gospel to be preached. Regardless of what is happening in the world that week, if you cannot or do not have the skill to connect it with the biblical message, stick with the Scripture proclaimed. Making references to current world events, issues of injustice, and other matters that can often weigh heavy in the hearts and minds of your congregation is vital, but it should be done within the context of the scriptures read and not detract from that core proclamation. Another important thing to remember is that a sermon is not the place for announcements, nor the place to promote your next Bible study series. It is certainly not the place to offer orientations about what people should do before, during, or after liturgy. It is not the time to teach a class about the days of Holy Week, for example. There are good adult education opportunities to accomplish that throughout the week.

On one particular Sunday, I decided to try something new to connect with my own congregation. I prepared my sermon and used my standard style of incorporating relevant humor, anecdotes, and inspirational images.[3] With all the research about contemporary minds and our capacity

3. The Rev. Albert R. Cutie, sermon for the Second Sunday in Lent, accessed March 12, 2013, https://www.youtube.com/watch?v=XGF4gV2NmcM.

to multi-task, I decided to add additional visuals. I used the screens at our contemporary service to project questions from my sermon outline while I was speaking. This kind of approach requires some coordination with those who handle projectors and sound equipment, but it can easily be integrated and helps to focus or emphasize to the listeners those concepts or ideas you are inviting them to contemplate within the sermon.

The response I got was what I expected. Only a group of young people came to me after the service and said, "Hey, Father, that was cool how the questions went up on the screen as you were speaking to us." Most of the adults did not mention it at all. Maybe many of them did not even notice, possibly because they may not be as accustomed to the interactive or multi-tasking approach of their younger counterparts in the congregation. The use of graphics or other interactive methods may still not be part of the communication culture of those in older demographics and church leaders must be aware of that. Where screens are appreciated in more contemporary style services, when it comes to traditional services and buildings, they can often be perceived as a nuisance.

I believe this sermon using the graphics and visual messages connected with the younger sector of our congregation because it incorporated an element of media they were not accustomed to seeing within the context of church. It brought the younger folks a bit of the multi-tasking they are accustomed to in their daily media interactions. In other words, sermons that connect require all the good stuff which is part of any good sermon in addition to a good dosage of creativity and risk-taking. Today's preacher continues trying new things, realizing that he or she is competing with a myriad of distractions present in the lives of most listeners.

If the way contemporary ears listen has changed, what could that reality be telling us about how preachers must preach? Let's consider a few areas that may help the twenty-first-century preacher reach his or her congregation more effectively.

The Enthusiasm Factor

For years I have been privileged to mentor and work with a variety of seminarians. Some time ago we had them come to our parish to preach and to speak about their journey as students of theology. My wife and I took them out to dinner and listened to them talk about the upcoming Super Bowl and the two teams involved. There was laughter, spontaneous interactions, intelligent conversations, and a good deal of debate across the table. Their voices were filled with conviction as they defended their team. It was indeed lively and extremely entertaining dialogue! After such a dynamic exchange, I looked forward to listening to their preaching and I was excited for our congregation.

The next morning, as those same seminarians took the pulpit and read through their well thought-out sermon texts, their tone and energy were totally different. It was

actually rather dry and dull. I am sure they did not mean
their sermons to come across that way, but those dynamic
personalities and spontaneous thoughts so clearly present
the night before were nowhere to be found in the pulpit the
next morning. I suspect they were just there to preach as
they had heard sermons preached before, and they appeared
to be satisfied with the results. Yet, for me, as someone who
had personally witnessed their dynamic personalities and
brilliant interactions at the dinner table the night before,
I was disappointed. Perhaps my greatest regret was that all
the enthusiasm they seemed to have for football could not
compare with their enthusiasm for the message they were
proclaiming. That *enthusiasm factor* which was so palpable
in their engaging exchanges about football was not present
at all when they were preaching. This was also the message
they are preparing to preach for the rest of their lives as
ministers in God's church—and they did not seem to be all
that enthusiastic about it. As clergy, we shy away from any
kind of negative review of another's pastoral work. So I did
exactly what most of us do and said absolutely nothing.

Yet, the fact remains that enthusiasm is contagious and it
cannot be faked. If we motivate our preachers to bring their
personalities with them to the pulpit and to show the same
kind of enthusiasm they so easily and spontaneously express
for other areas of life as they preach the gospel, I am convinced something great will begin to happen among clergy
and their congregations. I am not suggesting being cheery
and loud; how the preacher communicates their enthusiasm

for the message they are sharing is critical. Perhaps this is why I insist on the "enthusiasm factor" and why I believe it can be a real turning point that will help us renew the church and the craft of preaching in a way that very few other things can.

We have countless development programs in most of our mainstream denominations; institutions and special projects to help us plan and strategize for the future of changing congregations. We are certainly spending resources of time and money trying to figure out how to survive and/or thrive in an uncertain future. Yet, how much enthusiasm are we actually putting into the basics? In order to connect with twenty-first-century listeners, we must pay special attention to the sermon, the music, and the overall environment of the service. These are the basics that attract and keep people coming back for more. I am convinced that if we inject the enthusiasm factor into all these basics the result will be a church that speaks to people today and is not afraid to assume its missionary identity. For what is a missionary, if he or she is not one who does everything possible to connect with the culture, language, and customs that allow God's work to take place? Either we are totally committed to mission or we are not going to be around much longer. Many churches are shrinking and dying because they have not paid attention to the reality that surrounds them. We cannot afford to just "do what we've always done" and get away with it. A renewed enthusiasm for the Gospel mandate and the way we present it, must be at the heart of our activity as church.

The Creativity Factor

I learned a lot from an old priest who supervised me during one of my earliest field placements, at the beginning of my seminary years. He had a real missionary zeal and it was apparent that this led him to be a very effective instrument of evangelism and outreach for old and young alike. There was a lot that was "out of the box" in the way he approached ministry. He would often tell me, "Albert, if we keep doing what we are doing, we will keep getting what we are getting." That phrase has never left my mind. The fact is that in order to preach—as in any other area of ministry—we must be willing and ready to be creative. And so I present to you what I believe to be the *creativity factor* when it comes to preaching.

Like most other professionals, regardless of their field of expertise, I understand that preaching is a real craft and that those of us who become priests and preachers must take this craft very seriously, constantly working to improve. Yet, after several years of preaching regularly, I began to understand that effective preaching requires something more. Today's preacher must use a level of creativity that not only conveys the words and concepts, but makes them stick. Retention is one of our most significant challenges. In order for listeners to retain, the content of the sermon must be tied and clearly connected to something else, preferably something they will keep thinking about throughout the week. I spend quite a bit of time trying to find a simple story, an image, a joke, an inspiring anecdote—almost anything that will make the message resonate with the congregation. Sometimes the biblical message will require several anecdotes or stories that will serve as illustrations and/or connectors.

I am convinced that preachers cannot ignore the urgency of creative preparation and dynamic delivery as essential ingredients for effective preaching. We cannot simply settle for doing what comes naturally or within our own comfort zone. Contemporary preachers must be willing to be "out of the box" enough to make the message of the Word of God appealing and digestible for our people. Sometimes, just paying attention to what is happening around us provides opportunities to be more creative and dynamic in our approach. We must weave our God-given creativity into the fabric of our preaching in order to offer a message that excites others to follow. Throwing a bunch of disconnected theological ideas out there will not do it, regardless of how great that may have sounded to your preaching professor back in seminary.

Fans of late night television will remember David Letterman and his "Top 10 Lists." While I struggled to stay up that late, once I was hooked it was important to stay up because I did not want to miss that particular day's list. That kind of anticipation and expectation is priceless and not dissimilar to the anticipation people associate with going out of their way to visit a church because they know they will find preaching, music, or hospitality that are particularly appealing to them. Listeners of transformative and inspirational messages are always ready and willing to come back for more.

While I do not like to use gimmicks, shortly after Letterman's retirement my bishop invited me to be the preacher at the ordination service at our cathedral in Miami and I decided to share my own "Top 10 List" with a congregation composed of many clergy, several seminarians, others in the process of formation for ordination, family members, and, of course, the candidates about to be ordained. It was my attempt to make this as personable as possible. I prayed, asking God to guide me through the creation of my own list. It was my sincere hope that those to be ordained and those who loved them could take something with them to help them remember the grace of that day and the seriousness of the task at hand. It was not easy to limit my list to ten, but in order to make it happen, I knew I had to find a way to do it. So here it goes:

Top Ten List for a *Happy* and *Healthy* Ministry

1. Be flexible like the palm tree. When storms and hurricanes come, they know how to bend and that is why they survive.
2. Choose to always have the best experience regardless of where or in what particular context you are called to serve. It does not mean that you will always be paid well or appreciated, it just means you know how to make the *best* of each situation.

3. Prepare your sermon every time you preach! There is no greater sign of "Spiritual Malpractice" than submitting your people to a dull and unprepared sermon. And please, pray about your sermon before you preach it.

4. Remember John Donne: "No man is an island . . . . " Make it a priority to share and spend time with fellow clergy. Isolated clergy persons are usually frustrated ones—and we have already gone over the quota on those.

5. Never start your day, any meeting, or any function you lead without a moment of prayer. If you don't remind people about the presence of God, *who* will?

6. Listen, listen, and listen! Before you present your new or old congregation with your brilliant plan for them, first try to listen to what they have in mind. Listening is still the best way to learn.

7. Pray for your bishop. The size of his hat is usually symbolic of the size of the problems he deals with daily. Also, stay connected to the work of your diocese—beyond your own parish or particular ministry. Anglicans are not Congregationalists; we share the work of the diocese together.

8. Never stop being a student. Theology and ministry, like the rest of the world, evolve. You, too, are a professional that needs to "keep your license current." Read good books and don't limit yourself to churchy stuff.

9. Be mindful of the fact that the Holy Spirit has a tendency to be disorganized. Even when you have planned and prepared everything just the way you think it should

be, make sure you allow some room for the Holy Spirit
to work and to be spontaneous!

10. Know when you've done enough and always take care
of yourself. By taking your day off and taking care of
yourself and your family, you will model responsible
Christian behavior to your colleagues and to the people
you are called to serve.

While it is true that many times a joke, certain anecdotes, the use of an object or even a "list" can appear gimmicky, when these serve to make the biblical message more
incarnate in the reality of the congregation, creative instruments like these can be effective. Creativity can take many
other forms, as well. The important thing to keep in mind is
that whatever we do in preaching must be at the service of
the Word of God. If it detracts from the Word or the liturgy,
then you can be sure it is not the right kind of creativity.
Thus, the preacher must discern very carefully what kind of
creative elements will enhance his or her preaching. Taking
risks will always be a challenge, but some of those risks will
pay off. Allowing your creative juices to flow can only help
you become a better preacher and your congregation to
become better receptors of the message.

The Prayer Factor

Before a preacher begins to preach, it is important he or she
be aware of what the Holy Spirit could be inspiring us to

say on God's behalf. As William Brosend often says, every preacher must first answer what he calls the *homiletical question*: "What does the Holy Spirit want the people of God to hear from these texts on this occasion?" This is no easy task; it certainly requires much prayer and discernment.

We often talk about technique, delivery, and the effect of technology on our preaching, but a real preacher of the Gospel cannot forget that the most important part of the craft of preaching is proclaiming God's Word in a way that it is always God's. Praying the sermon is essential. The time we spend praying the lessons from the Scriptures assigned to us for a given celebration is never wasted time. Our congregants deserve a sermon that has been the product of real prayer and study.

The actual practice of "praying the sermon" is something that begins as close to Monday as possible. This will allow you sufficient time to soak in the lessons and truly pray with them. Every preacher has his or her preference when it comes to sermon preparation, but being committed to the prayer factor is a process which takes a lifetime. The more we practice it, the more we will appreciate it. The experienced preacher realizes that it is only by God's grace that the sermon can actually touch the hearts and challenge the minds of God's people. When you pray your sermon well, your preaching usually goes very well.

The one hundredth Archbishop of Canterbury, Michael Ramsey, would often speak of the role of priest as being one who must be "with God with the people on your heart." This popular Ramsey phrase speaks to me of what is essential in praying the sermon and in the importance of Brosend's homiletical question. Are we truly listening for the Holy Spirit's guidance on what these particular biblical lessons are saying to those entrusted to our spiritual care?

For all these reasons, the dedicated preacher of the Gospel must begin the week by praying the Scriptures, allowing God to speak first. When we pray our sermons, people sense that this is God's work taking place and not just our own. The preacher that truly prays his or her sermon, will not go wrong.

The Structure / Content Factor

I'll never forget the old lady who once told me, "The pastor's sermons are good, but he has one problem, he never knows how to land the plane." Sounds funny, but it is too often the case that preachers tend to preach what seem to be "eternal" and never-ending sermons. This is what usually goes on: A good sermon gets going, people are into it, and the preacher is into it. It is getting the job done. Yet, as the sermon gets close to the perfect place to end, the preacher takes off again or—even worse—the sermon goes into a holding pattern and now nobody knows where it is going. At that point listeners are lost, people are looking at their watches, and instead of moving hearts, the length of the sermon begins to remind people they are seated on a hard wood pew. Sound familiar?

One common complaint in sermon evaluations is that the sermon had no clear structure. Often you will hear people say, "That sermon was all over the place." Like those classic essays we learned to write in school, a sermon needs an introduction, a body, and a conclusion. If any of those elements are not clear from the beginning, listeners quickly become lost, spending too much energy figuring out where the message is going and where it came from. It is best to use an outline and never feel you must cover the entire history of salvation in one sermon. The trick is to remember that most good sermons are meant to be incomplete; a good preacher motivates listeners to complete the sermon in their daily lives. Important questions can remain open-ended and unanswered, and a sense of deep personal reflection should occupy the hearts and minds of those who experienced the preaching of the Word.

While there is often a significant amount of hesitation among younger people in the church, especially those in the process of formation for ministry, toward the use of story-telling, humor, or spontaneity in sermons, today's church must be humble enough to recognize that Jesus himself did all that he could to use stories, examples, and real life experiences. None of it was "dumbing down," but all of it was certainly connecting. Jesus used those instruments because they worked—and they still do. Just imagine the Bible without those powerful parables and images from everyday living. So much of what Jesus used in his preaching and teaching was earthy and easy to grasp. Much of what he said was clearly connected to the context of his listeners. If as a preacher of the gospel you are prompted to talk about Trinitarian *perichoresis* in a sermon, you have to ask yourself if you are doing this for yourself or whether you are really committed to preach the Gospel in a way that is accessible and inspiring to all.

There can be elements of both content and structure that can be useless and out of place. Usually, your own theological musings and the lingo you discovered in seminary do not belong in the sermon. When it comes to preaching, I believe in the popular axiom, "Less is more." Clarity and simplicity are both virtues we find in Jesus; virtues we should all emulate as preachers. One of the premises I use in preparation is that if my grandma couldn't understand it, I shouldn't say it. My grandmother was a person who wanted to pray and be renewed by her experience at church. She did not want the priest offering a theology class or using terminology she was never going to understand. She just wanted to be a good Christian—a good follower of Jesus Christ.

My point here is that a sermon with a clear structure and truly accessible content is a sermon that can be easily followed, flowing in a way that brings the message alive, clearly explicating the practical application of the biblical texts. Good sermons are not like pulling wisdom teeth, where the listeners must really reach to depths of his or her imagination in order to follow the homily. Ambiguity in theological matters can be challenging and imaginative—even exciting in an academic setting. Yet, when it comes to preaching it can be a real source of frustration to a congregation. In the practice of preaching, leave some of that ambiguity behind, and aim to bring clarity and inspiration to your homily. The preacher must always remember it is about them—the people of God—not about you.

Study Questions

1. Do you remember a time when a specific sermon really connected with you? How did you respond to it? Can you give examples of preaching that did not connect? How did you respond to it?
2. What factors do you consider most important in preaching today? How important do you consider Enthusiasm, Creativity and Prayer to the craft of preaching today?
3. Content and Structure are vital to the transmission of any message. What role do they have in homiletics/ preaching?

CONCLUSION

A Call within a Call—
Preacher as Communicator

"Take advantage of every opportunity to practice your communication skills so that when important occasions arise, you will have the gift, the style, the sharpness, the clarity, and the emotions to affect other people."

—JIM ROHN

Every time we preach, it is indeed an "important occasion." The opportunity and privilege of preaching cannot be taken lightly; I am sure no serious preacher does. The church has been given the sacred task to communicate the most important message of all: the Gospel of our Lord Jesus Christ. Rapid developments in technology and changes in communication methodology, both in our speaking and in our listening, offer us great challenges and great opportunities. When preachers go out of their way to connect effectively, speak professionally and clearly, and prepare a well structured and well thought out sermon, they are responding to the needs of today's listeners. When we ignore these basic elements, we will have a hard time connecting.

It is no secret that most denominations lack new members, and a significant number are just struggling to survive. We see too many churches with a declining, aging membership, and we wonder what we can do to get new people in the door. Dioceses, clergy, and lay leaders invest time and economic resources to find creative ways of attracting new members and that is all very good. We must continue to do all of that, because it matters and, in the long term, it will make a difference.

Yet, I am convinced that the secret to church growth and to creating truly vibrant churches is in the quality and connectedness of the preaching. How much effort are we putting into preaching excellence; into spreading the Good News with a renewed sense of enthusiasm and in a way that pays attention to the way contemporary audiences listen? We must begin to humbly accept that in almost every area of communications, we are not keeping up with the world around us.

Megachurches are not filled with people who came from a vacuum. Most of them were baptized and probably even raised in one of our mainstream churches. Sure, many of them still love the old hymns, the sacramental rites, and the liturgy; most will tell you they never really planned on moving on from the tradition of their upbringing. However, if you ask the great majority of them why they left, almost universally the answer will be, "I was bored," or "I got nothing out of it." If we translate that to church talk, it usually means just one thing: the sermon did not connect with me and I found nothing that I could take home with me to motivate and strengthen my desire to live the Christian life. As N.T. Wright observed:

> Our culture is moving in all kinds of ways toward a post-post-modernism that has yet to be shaped but for which our public world longs as it lurches from boredom and trivia to dangerous and dehumanizing behavior. I have argued that the God of the Bible, and especially of the Gospels, can be understood only as God-in-public. . . . We face a challenging possibility in our generation: to move beyond the sterile alternatives of different types of post-Enlightenment tyranny on one hand—the fundamentalism and secularism that have so often slugged it out on the spurious battleground of ideologically driven would-be exegesis—and postmodern chaos on the other.[1]

The great Mother Teresa of Calcutta often spoke of the time she became aware that she was experiencing "a call within a call." She had already given her life to Jesus at a very young age when she entered the convent to become a nun

---

1. N.T. Wright, *Surprised by Scripture* (New York: HarperCollins, 2014), 180.

and teach wealthy school girls. One day, as she took the train for her annual spiritual retreat, there was something else she began to hear from God. She explains how she began to feel "a call within her call." Sister Teresa understood that it was God's will for her to leave the comfortable setting of her convent and the school girls she taught and she was to go out into the streets of Calcutta—one of the poorest regions of the world—in order to work and live among the poorest of the poor. That call came within another call that was already being responded to with fidelity. Yet, this new call required its own urgent response.

Today's preachers must be willing to hear a "call within their call." I believe the call God is making to the church is for us to become better communicators in an age of constant communication. If we have a passion for the Gospel and its saving message, we must then be willing to be passionate and professional communicators. It is a matter of hearing the urgent call of God who is inviting us to live and work within our second call. We cannot ignore it. There is an urgent need for bridge builders who can master this new language and who are seeking to find new means by which to connect. The church cannot stay on the sidelines, arms folded, and watching it all go by. In order to preach the good news effectively to the people of this specific time and place, we must become master communicators, obtaining whatever skills, techniques, and knowledge are within our reach—and we must do it with courage and enthusiasm—for the greater Glory of God.

APPENDIX I

Survey of Preachers

Survey for Preachers: on the Impact of New Media and Changes in the Listening Context on Preaching[2]

There are three questions below. This survey should not take you more than three to five minutes to complete. The goal of the survey is to explore among one hundred preachers and one hundred listeners of sermons what level of impact they perceive new forms of media, and the constantly changing "listening context" in our society have on the craft of preaching today.

Using scale from 1–10 (1—*no impact*; 5—*some impact*; and 10—*significant impact*)

---

2. Survey created and written by The Rev. Dr. Albert R. Cutié.

1. In your perception as a preacher, how do new forms of media (i.e., Internet, social media, mobile phones, tablets, etc.) impact your listeners and the listening context? *(Rate impact of new forms of media on how your sermon is received by today's listeners.)* _____

2. In your delivery and preparation as a preacher, what impact do these new forms of media have on your content and approach to preaching? *(Rate how new forms of media impact your style of preaching and your sermon preparation.)* _____

3. In my personal experience as a preacher, I would say the overall impact new forms of media have on my preaching experience is *(Rate how new forms of media impact your overall approach to the craft of preaching—especially your particular listeners and preaching style.)* _____

APPENDIX II

Survey of Listeners

Survey for Those Who Listen to Sermons with Regularity: on the Impact of New Media and Changes in the Listening Context on Preaching

Using scale from 1–10 (1—*no impact*; 5—*some impact* and 10—*significant impact*)

1. As a congregant and hearer of sermons, how and to what extent do new forms of media (i.e., Internet, social media, mobile phones, tablets, etc.) impact the way you listen to a sermon? *(Rate impact of new forms of media on the way you listen to the sermons you hear.)* _____

2. As an active listener to sermons, what impact do you perceive these new forms of media have on your preacher's approach to the craft of preaching? *(Rate how you perceive new forms of media impact your preacher's content, delivery and/or sermon preparation.)*   _____

3. In my personal experience, as a regular listener of sermons, I would say the overall impact new forms of media have on the way I listen to and receive sermons is *(Rate how new forms of media impact your overall approach to listening to sermons.)*   _____

APPENDIX III

Sermon Evaluation

You are invited to evaluate the sermon you will hear today. Please follow the instructions below. Thank you!

(Use numbers from 1–10. 1—"I disagree," 10—"I totally agree")

1. *Do not fill out the form until you have heard the <u>entire</u> sermon.*
2. *Please refrain from answering each category until the preacher has finished.*
3. *Fold and place in envelope.*
4. *Seal and drop in the offering plate.*

  1. The sermon was ***interesting*** and caught my attention.   _____
  2. The ***biblical message*** from today's lessons was presented with clarity.   _____

3. The **structure and content** of the sermon were easy to grasp.   _____

4. **God's Word** was proclaimed through this sermon.   _____

5. The preacher appeared **interested in conveying a message of faith** to me.   _____

6. This sermon **inspired me to live as a better disciple.**   _____

7. I am **motivated in my faith** and I feel ready **to do something for God.**   _____

8. This sermon **challenged me and made me think.**   _____

9. The **voice of the preacher was easy to hear and understand.**   _____

10. I was able **to see and hear the preacher well.**   _____

Bibliography

Baehr, Theodore. *Getting the Word Out: How to Communicate the Gospel in Today's World*. San Francisco: Harper & Row Publishers, 1986.

Beebe, Steven A., and Susan J Beebe. *Public Speaking: An Audience-Centered Approach*. 9th edition. Upper Saddle River, NJ: Pearson, 2015.

Brosend, William. *The Preaching of Jesus: Gospel Proclamation, Then and Now*. Louisville, KY: Westminster John Knox Press, 2010.

Campbell, Heidi A. *Digital Religion: Understanding Religious Practice in New Media Worlds*. New York: Routledge, 2013.

Carr, Nicholas. *What the Internet is doing to our Brains*. New York: W.W. Norton & Company, 2011.

Dargan, Edwin C., and Ralph G. Turnbull. *A History of Preaching*. Grand Rapids, MI: Baker Book House, 1974.

Duduit, Michael, ed. *Communicate with Power: Insights from America's Top Communicators.* Grand Rapids, MI: Baker Books, 1996.

Elliott, Mark Barger. *Creative Styles of Preaching.* Louisville, KY: John Knox Press, 2000.

Erickson, Millard J., and James L. Heflin. *Old Wine in New Wineskins: Doctrinal Preaching in a Changing World.* Grand Rapids, MI: Baker Books, 1997.

Gali, Mark, and Craig Brian Larson. *Preaching that Connects: Using the Techniques of Journalists to Add Impact to Your Sermons.* Grand Rapids: Zondervan Publishing House, 1994.

Gregory the Great. "The Book of Pastoral Rule, Part III, 1-3, translated by James Barmby," *A Select Library of Nicene and Post-Nicene Fathers of the Christian Church, Vol. XII.* New York: The Christian Literature Company, 1894.

Henderson, David W. *Culture Shift: Communicating God's Truth to our Changing World.* Grand Rapids, MI: Baker Books, 1998.

Hipps, Shane. *Flickering Pixels: How Technology Shapes Your Faith.* Grand Rapids, MI: Zondervan, 2009.

Hybels, Bill, Stuart Briscoe, and Haddon Robinson. *Mastering Contemporary Preaching.* Portland, OR: Multnomah, 1989.

Johnston, Graham. *Preaching to a Postmodern World: A Guide to Reaching Twenty-First Century Listeners.* Grand Rapids, MI: Baker Books, 2001.

Kraft, Charles H. *Communication Theory for Christian Witness.* Revised edition. New York: Orbis Books, 1991.

Larsen, David L. *The Anatomy of Preaching: Identifying the Issues in Preaching Today*. Grand Rapids, MI: Baker Book House, 1989.

Lischer, Richard. *Theories of Preaching: Selected Readings in the Homiletical Tradition*. Durham, NC: Labyrinth Press, 1987.

Lloyd-Jones, D. Martyn. *Preaching and Preachers*. Grand Rapids, MI: Zondervan Publishing House, 1972.

Logan, Samuel T., Jr., ed. *The Preacher and Preaching: Reviving the Art in the Twentieth Century*. Phillipsburg, NJ: Presbyterian and Reformed Publishing Company, 1986.

Long, Thomas G. *The Witness of Preaching*. Louisville: Westminster/John Knox Press, 1989.

Meyrowitz, Joshua. *No Sense of Place: The Impact of Electronic Media on Social Behavior.* New York: Oxford University Press, 1985.

Miller, Calvin. *The Empowered Communicator: The 7 Keys to Unlocking an Audience.* Nashville, TN: Broadman & Holman Publishers, 1994.

Mueller, Pam, and Oppenheimer, Daniel. "The Pen is Mightier than the Keyboard: Advantages of Longhand Over Laptop Note Taking. *Psychological Science, Vol 15*(6), (April 23, 2014): 1159–68. Accessed March 12, 2015. http://pss.sagepub.com/content/early/2014/04/22/0956 797614524581.full.pdf+html.

Ong, Walter J. *Orality and Literacy: The Technologizing of the Word*. New York: Methuen, 2014.

————. *Rhetoric, Romance, and Technology: Studies in the Interaction of Expression and Culture*. New York: Cornell University Press, 2012.

Quicke, Michael J. *360 Degree Preaching: Hearing, Speaking and Living the Word*. Grand Rapids, MI: Baker Academic, 2003.

Rogness, Michael. *Preaching to a TV Generation: The Sermon in the Electronic Age*. Lima, OH: CSS Publishing, 1994.

Roland, Jarod L., Hacker, Carl D., Breshears, Jonathan D., Gaona, Charles M., Hogan, R. Edward, Burton, Harold, Corbetta, Maurizio, and Leuthardt, Eric C. "Brain Mapping." *Frontiers in Human Neuroscience*. July 31, 2013. http://journal.frontiersin.org/article/10.3389/fnhum .2013.00431/full. Accessed October 5, 2014.

Rueter, Alvin C. *Making Good Preaching Better: A Step-by-Step Guide to Scripture-Based, People-Centered Preaching*. Collegeville, MN: The Liturgical Press, 1997.

Schnapp, Diana Corley. "Listening in Spirituality and Religion," in *Listening and Human Communication in the 21st Century*, edited by Andrew D. Wolvin. Malden, MA: Blackwell Publishing, 2010.

Sheen, Fulton J. *Treasure in Clay: The Autobiography of Archbishop Fulton J. Sheen*. New York: Images Publishing Group, 1982.

Simmons, Martha J., ed. *Preaching on the Brink: The Future of Homiletics*. Nashville, TN: Abingdon Press, 1996.

Sugden, Edward H., ed. *Wesley's Standard Sermons Consisting of 44 Discourses Published in Four Volumes: Vol. 1, Preface*. London: Epworth Press, 1956.

Van Harn, Roger E. *Pew Rights: For People Who Listen to Sermons*. Grand Rapids, MI: William B. Eerdermans Publishing Company, 1992.

Webb, Joseph M. *Comedy and Preaching*. St. Louis, MO: Chalice Press.

————. 2001. *Preaching without Notes*. Nashville, TN: Abingdon Press, 1998.

Wells, C. Richard, and A. Boyd Luter. *Inspired Preaching*. Nashville, TN: Broadman Press, 2002.

White, L. Michael. *The Social Origins of Christian Architecture*. Cambridge, MA: Harvard Theological Studies, 1996.

Willimon, William H. *Preaching and Leading Worship*. Appendix. Philadelphia: Westminster Press, 1984.

————. "The Preacher as an Extension of the Preaching Moment," in *Preaching on the Brink: The Future of Preaching*, edited by Martha J. Simmons. Nashville, TN: Abingdon Press, 1996.

Willimon, William H., and Richard Lischer. *Concise Encyclopedia of Preaching*. Louisville: Westminster John Knox Press, 1995.

Wilson-Kastner, Patricia. *Imagery for Preaching*. Minneapolis, MN: Fortress Press, 1989.

Wilson, Paul S. *A Concise History of Preaching*. Nashville, TN: Abingdon Press, 1992.

Wolvin, Andrew D., ed. *Listening and Human Communication in the 21st Century*. Malden, MA: Blackwell Publishing, 2010.

Wright, N.T. *Surprised by Scripture: Engaging Contemporary Issues*. New York: HarperCollins, 2014.

Xhu, Erping, Matthew Kaplan, R. Charles Dershimer, and Inger Bergom. "Use of Laptops in the Classroom: Research and Best Practices." *CRLT Occasional Papers*, no. 30. University of Michigan, 2011.

www.ingramcontent.com/pod-product-compliance
Lightning Source LLC
Jackson TN
JSHW011404130125
77033JS00023B/840